"This remarkable book tells the story of the Brethren in Christ not as a dusty denominational history but as a living testimony to God's revitalizing Spirit. Focused enough to capture the essential biblical values that unite, it is also comprehensive enough to convey the scope of God's global church. Full of practical wisdom and written with enthusiastic urgency, this book will inform and inspire you to worship God afresh and to participate in Christ's mission with renewed vigor."

WALTER KIM, president of the National Association of Evangelicals

"Many voices in gracious conversation, poignant stories and examples of how core values translate into practice, and a powerful blending of Anabaptist and Pietist spirituality. This is a rich resource, not only for the global Brethren in Christ community, but for any follower of Jesus willing to exhibit the 'generous curiosity' about discipleship, mission, and church that the editors commend."

STUART MURRAY, founding director of the Centre for Anabaptist Studies and author of *The New Anabaptists*

"This new collection of essays aptly demonstrates how the ten Brethren in Christ core values that were first articulated in North America translate well in different cultural contexts. With an international cast of contributors, the essays explore historic Brethren in Christ theology and practice, emphasize the church as a worldwide community, and tell the real-life stories of fellow believers around the world who have faithfully lived out the core values. Together, these essays offer a richly textured mosaic of cultures bound together by a common mission to share the good news of Jesus with the world."

HARRIET SIDER BICKSLER, editor for the Brethren in Christ Historical Society and editor of *Shalom! A Journal for the Practice of Reconciliation*

"*Compelling Convictions* is a gift for the Brethren in Christ church and for the world! While our Brethren in Christ core values represent timeless biblical priorities, these fresh reflections written by brothers and sisters from around the world will encourage, inspire, and challenge us to consider how we apply these values to our lives today."

HEATHER BEATY, bishop of the Brethren in Christ Susquehanna Conference

"Written from an Anabaptist perspective, *Compelling Convictions* provides values that inspire and encourage individuals to act with creative faith in the present-day world. The discussion includes voices from the global BIC church, engaging us in our unique contexts without creating boundaries that include or exclude people. I highly recommend this book!"

CÉSAR GARCÍA, general secretary of Mennonite World Conference

"Creeds, catechisms, confessions, and core values have long been recognized as statements that unify the church around central pillars and beliefs. This book carries on that important tradition in providing a guiding light for the global BIC family. Against a backdrop of polarization and fragmentation in our world, the writers have articulated and affirmed these cherished values that hold us together."

TODD LESTER, director of leadership and global programs for Be In Christ Church of Canada

compelling convictions

compelling convictions

FINDING
OUR FUTURE
IN A
MODERN WORLD

BRETHREN IN CHRIST CORE VALUES REVISITED

Edited
by
Terry L.
BRENSINGER
Jennifer
LANCASTER
Alan
ROBINSON

HERALD
PRESS

Harrisonburg, Virginia

Herald Press
PO Box 866, Harrisonburg, Virginia 22803
www.HeraldPress.com

Library of Congress Cataloging-in-Publication Data
Names: Brensinger, Terry L., editor.
Title: Compelling convictions : finding our future in a modern world
  (brethren in Christ core values revisited) / Terry L. Brensinger [and
  two others].
Description: Harrisonburg, Virginia : Herald Press, [2024] | Includes
  bibliographical references.
Identifiers: LCCN 2024005629 (print) | LCCN 2024005630 (ebook) | ISBN
  9781513813622 (paper) | ISBN 9781513813639 (hc) | ISBN 9781513813646
  (ebooks)
Subjects: LCSH: Brethren in Christ Church--United States. | BISAC: RELIGION
  / Christian Ministry / Discipleship | RELIGION / Christian Rituals &
  Practice / General
Classification: LCC BX9675.A43 U58 2024 (print) | LCC BX9675.A43 (ebook)
  | DDC 289.7/73--dc23/eng/20240429
LC record available at https://lccn.loc.gov/2024005629
LC ebook record available at https://lccn.loc.gov/2024005630

Study guides are available for many Herald Press titles at www.HeraldPress.com.

COMPELLING CONVICTIONS
© 2024 by General Conference of the Brethren in Christ. Released by Herald Press.
  All rights reserved.
Library of Congress Control Number: 2024005629
International Standard Book Number: 978-1-5138-1362-2 (paperback);
  978-1-5138-1363-9 (hardcover); 978-1-5138-1364-6 (ebook)
Printed in United States of America

28 27 26 25 24   10 9 8 7 6 5 4 3 2 1

Table of Contents

Foreword

He called the crowd with his disciples, and said to them, "If any want to become my followers, let them deny themselves and take up their cross and follow me. For those who want to save their life will lose it, and those who lose their life for my sake, and for the sake of the gospel, will save it." (Mark 8:34–35)

With this statement, Jesus was clear, very clear about the radical nature of the kingdom of God. At the same time, his words were confusing—what does it mean to say that we lose what we save, and that we save what we lose? How can such clarity also be confusing? Perhaps it is because to us this idea is both counterintuitive and countercultural. But this is what Jesus said, and what he invites us, his followers, into. His counterintuitive and countercultural teaching also raises important questions for us: From where do we derive our identity? And how is our life being shaped? As Brethren in Christ, our core values help us ground our identity in Christ. As these values are lived out, they shape us to be citizens of the kingdom of God.

The first followers of Jesus lived in a vastly different world from ours. Our world has experienced unprecedented levels of social change. The world has changed—is changing—and the pace of change itself is accelerating, seemingly day by day. Amid rapid change, we often look for meaning and significance in things that are not ultimate. These non-ultimate systems and structures shape us to be and live in ways that look more like conformity to the world rather than the counterintuitive and countercultural kingdom of God.

Is it possible to break free from this powerful, value-shaping, and life-shaping world? Is it possible for the followers of Jesus to be so deeply and thoroughly transformed that we are shaped by the kingdom of God rather than shaped by the world? Thankfully, we know that it is. This transformation occurs as the values by which we live lead us to lose our lives rather than engage in the futility of trying to save them.

This book is an invitation to reflect on the Brethren in Christ core values by listening to the voices of others. The thirty-six contributing voices in this book represent Brethren in Christ brothers and sisters across eight countries. We are deeply grateful for their witness and their willingness to contribute strong theological and biblical descriptions of the values while also offering personal and communal lived-out experiences of these values.

As the Brethren in Christ approaches its 250th year, this book acknowledges both how we are shaped by our past and how we desire to shape our future. We hope that you, the reader, will have ears to hear, and that you will hear, engage, reflect, and then commune with others who are also on this journey. In doing this, each of us can experience transformation in our way of being in this world.

—Terry L. Brensinger, Jennifer Lancaster,
and Alan Robinson, editors

Introduction

According to the sign adjacent to its main entrance, the Brethren in Christ Choma Secondary School in southern Zambia exists "to provide a pupil with an environment for spiritual, academic, physical and moral growth." Year after year, companies, organizations, churches and schools around the world spend considerable time and money developing such mission statements and identifying their core values. Why? Because, in the words of one writer for Forbes, values are "the 'guiding light' that steers the company's attitude and behavior towards others."[1] Values reinforce a sense of identity and history. Values create a positive and engaging atmosphere among the employees, volunteers and other stakeholders. Values inspire creativity and constructive initiatives.

Yet just as often, those same values ring hollow, eventually taking up more space on placards than in people's hearts, minds, and actions. A few years ago, one of us had dinner at Kennedy's Grill in Marlborough, Massachusetts. Before even sitting down, he noticed that every member of the restaurant staff was wearing a black t-shirt with the following slogan written in white letters across the back: "Kennedy's. . . Then. . . Now. . . Always." Out of curiosity, he asked his server—a senior member of the staff—what the words meant. "I have no idea," she politely responded. "The owners want us to wear them." This woman is hardly alone in articulating such a position. A 2017 Gallup survey found that only 27 percent of employees in the United States strongly agreed that they believe in their organization's values, while even fewer (23 percent) felt the same way about their ability to apply those values to their everyday work.[2] As Ron Carucci wrote about that poll in the Harvard Business Review, "Company value statements often become nothing more than cosmetic window dressing."[3]

FORMULATING OUR CORE VALUES

Remarkably, more than twenty years have passed since a group of Brethren in Christ (BIC) pastors, educators, administrators, and lay people met to formulate core values for our church in North America. Following four days of invigorating discussions, civil disagreements, and intense prayer, a sense of calmness came over the group. Before us were ten core values with which we all resonated. "This is who we are," we said to each other, "and this is who we aspire to be." Those same ten core values were later affirmed by the North American church and thoughtfully discussed in the book *Focusing Our Faith: Brethren in Christ Core Values*. This book, popular among BIC people across the United States and Canada, has served us well, both in terms of nurturing those within our community as well as sharing our faith with those outside.

Three important factors, however, have prompted BIC leaders to commission an entirely new book on our core values. First, although the core values were originally formulated by and for the BIC in North America, they soon gained wide acceptance by members of the global church. In spite of certain cultural and contextual differences, these core values resonate deeply with BIC people everywhere. As one young man from Zimbabwe commented, "these values are biblical and universally true." Because of this widening acceptance of the core values, we want a book that more fully represents the Brethren in Christ Church around the world.

As a result, essays in this book reflect BIC voices from many countries. If the young Zimbabwean is correct, then these essays will display the universality of how these values are lived out in BIC contexts throughout the world. We will hear from BIC people around the globe sharing their experiences of how the values are expressed in their culture at this particular moment. Paying attention to the global voice allows us to hear how cultural and contextual differences positively contribute to our identity as a whole.

Second, a great deal has taken place during the last twenty years, including the continuing decline of the church in the West; dynamic social movements for racial, gender, and economic justice; vast advances in technology; and a worldwide pandemic. With so much happening on both the national and international stages, it seems vital that we as BIC prayerfully reflect, not only on our core values and their application, but on the role that they might play in helping our churches engage a dramatically new social context. Are these values merely sentimental slogans like the one at Kennedy's Grill, or do they constitute compelling convictions, genuine "guiding lights" orienting us and motivating our mission in a rapidly changing world? The answer to that all-important question depends largely on how we use them.

The last changing factor is the voices themselves. In addition to the book becoming global, a new generation of writers has come about. Many of these voices are not historic to the BIC, as is the case in the original book, *Focusing Our Faith*. Rather, as the BIC family welcomes people from differing theological backgrounds, the shape of our identity expands along with it. This new generation of writers contributes both to the breadth of the values' expression and to our ability to be held together by this set of core values.

How should we begin to contemplate using our core values effectively? As an important but easily overlooked starting point, we believe that doing so requires both an understanding of contemporary social issues and an awareness of their potential implications for the church (1 Chronicles 12:32; Luke 12:54–56). In his widely read lecture *Science as a Vocation*, the sociologist Max Weber argued that while sociology cannot (at least explicitly) tell us how to feel about or respond to the world's problems, it can give us a clearer sense of what those problems are. The reverse could be said of our core values. While they do not identify the specific issues facing humanity, they do provide vision and hope for engaging them. For our values to fully germinate—or as Jesus put it, when likening the kingdom of heaven to yeast in Matthew 13, work their way all the way through the dough—we believe that both values and knowledge are essential. Values without knowledge lead to sentimental disengagement. Knowledge without values leads to moral chaos.

The work of the church is simply too important to perform haphazardly. While it is true that the Holy Spirit guides, teaches and empowers, it is no less true that the Spirit gifts and equips us to serve responsibly and effectively. We are reminded of a quote from the late Abraham Joshua Heschel, the great Jewish theologian/philosopher. What he says of individuals is certainly true of communities:

Man is constantly producing words and deeds, giving them over either to God or to the forces of evil. Every move, every detail, every act, every effort to match the spiritual and the material, is serious. The world is not a derelict; life is not a neutral ground. In this life of ours, the undirected goes astray, the haphazard becomes chaotic, what is left to chance is abandoned.[4]

Our core values can help us clarify who we are and what we will embody to the world. While never using them as boundaries to include and exclude people, these values are guideposts that point us toward greater intimacy with God and more faithful service to the world.

HOW TO READ THIS BOOK

We invite you to engage the values and these essays as a collective expression offering purpose and direction to our life as BIC. At best, these essays are the beginning of a conversation. They are not intended to say everything about our values. Instead, they are intended to spark creativity and conversation as we engage them together, as the local, national, and global BIC.

The BIC are at its best in conversation—when we listen intently to one another and seek understanding leading to more faithful discipleship. As you read, notice the tone of both authors and responding writers. Notice their graciousness toward one another and the postures with which they approach their writing. How might we take up such a generous curiosity in our local, national, and global contexts?

Conversation surrounding the core values will continue long after the publication of this book. We hope that these essays prompt conversation with attentiveness to fully recognize the depth and breadth of the values. As we engage together in practice, we begin to embody the values in ways that reinforce our identity and point to the beautiful diversity displayed in our BIC tradition.

Earlier we asked whether our core values were sentimental slogans or compelling convictions. To answer that question, one must first answer this one: "What distinguishes a sentimental slogan from a compelling conviction?" Is it the intrinsic truthfulness or force of the words themselves? That is, are certain words or phrases so powerful that to read them or hear them is to be changed? Or is it the manner and extent to which those words are practiced? Clearly, while the truthfulness of the words themselves is unarguably important, countless true phrases and statements have been carefully crafted and marketed throughout the world. They have also been forgotten. Why? No one bothered to use them. No one hung them on their doorposts or taught them to their children. No one asked, "What difference might these core values make in the way we live our lives, operate our schools, run our businesses, or build the church?"

As BIC, we have invested significant time and resources to write a meaningful mission statement, develop catchy branding slogans, and identify what we believe to be truly compelling core values. We have also dabbled with those values, referring to them from time to time and even preaching occasional sermons on one or two. What remains for us now is to unleash our creative energies, roll up our sleeves, and put these core values to good use. Our hope and prayer is that this book will help all of us as BIC to do just that.

CHAPTER 1

Experiencing God's Love and Grace

Antonio Gonzalez

We value the free gift of salvation in Christ Jesus
and the transforming power of the Holy Spirit.

INTRODUCTION: A PEOPLE OF EXPERIENCE

In the sixteenth century, the Spanish reformer Juan de Valdés wrote that regarding spiritual matters one matures to the measure of one's experiences, because in the spiritual life "everything is experience."[1] Most certainly, the BIC could make Juan de Valdés's affirmation their own. Throughout their history, the BIC have understood that faith is based on the actual experience of the grace of God and not on norms or doctrines.

The BIC church originated among Pennsylvania Anabaptists during the eighteenth century, individuals who experienced anew that they were lost but had been found. If the Anabaptists of the sixteenth century had understood justification as a new birth, the pietistic revival allowed them to personally experience this new birth. Along the bank of the Susquehanna

River they joyfully received forgiveness and mercy from Jesus, were baptized, and began a life of discipleship in community. As they wrote in their first Confession of Faith:

> . . . but to reveal this in us there appeared the healing Grace of God to convict us and to teach us that we confess that we have by nature a heart averse from God, devious and sinful. If this is confessed and acknowledged, it works a regret and sorrow and . . . the Light reveals to us the Fall into which Adam and we all have fallen; and this causes a longing, a praying, a weeping, and a calling to the promised Savior, to the World-Messiah. . . . Into such an open, poor sinner's heart the Lord Jesus will and can come, holding the communion meal; but that is, to bestow comfort, peace, love and trust. Then the record of sin as well as the guilt of Adam is stricken out, he receives comfort and forgiveness of sins and eternal life. A poor sinner feels and experiences that: and there the living Faith has its beginning, for Faith is a positive confidence . . . when the poor sinner offers himself obediently and subjects himself to live for the Lord Jesus and to be true from now on—to the One who has accepted him in adoption.[2]

From their point of view, the church should be comprised of those who truly experienced a call of God. It would be incorrect to see the first Anabaptists as fundamentalists who simply sought a literal obedience to Scripture. Neither were they liberals who only wanted to break away from the established order. The Anabaptists had personally experienced a new birth, seen their lives radically transformed by God, and demonstrated the gifts of the Holy Spirit. That was the real reason for wanting to faithfully obey God, which in turn led to their seeing the need to break away from the established order.

From their point of view, the church should be a community of believers who had experienced a personal revelation of God's love and grace.

The experience of God's love and grace constitutes the very foundation of Christianity. Without that experience, the church of God could not have been built. In reality, only God allows us to experience Jesus as the Messiah, and to acknowledge him as our King and Lord. This is not about a simple sentimental or subjective experience, but rather a divine revelation. Without it, the church is a work of flesh and blood, not a work of God. The apostle Paul wrote that the light that shone on the first day of creation is the same light that shines in the hearts of believers (2 Corinthians 4:6). The BIC have their origin in the search for a genuine experience of salvation, an experience that allows the establishment of a church of believers transformed by the grace of Jesus.

Alternatively, throughout history, Christians have attempted to impose themselves as a religion in a particular territory, either through the support of state powers, or with weaponized force. This in fact is what occurred in many parts of Europe and was implemented by Western colonizers in Latin America and other places in the world. Churches are then established, and membership is assured through the practice of certain religious rituals. Everyone that is born in that area goes on to be baptized and is considered Christian. It could also be that all who accept determined doctrines, or repeat a given confession of faith, are automatically considered "believers."

This is not something that happened only in the past. Today, we see examples of people who are proclaimed "saved" simply for having participated in a specific ritual or repeated some words having nothing to do with their experience and personal decision. Local congregations meet for many different reasons, but this does not always mean that there is a true revelation of God in their hearts leading to an authentic confession of faith. As BIC, with our heartfelt Pietist leanings and our Anabaptist obedience, we attempt to dismiss ritualistic religion in order to obey and experience God.

TESTIMONY: GRACE AND SUFFERING

Maricela and her husband arrived in Spain a few months before the 2020 pandemic. They were not just looking for better jobs. For several years, they had been trying to have children, and different treatments were tried, with no success. In Spain, they hoped to be able to work and pay for an expensive fertility treatment. The church met them during those difficult days, and helped them in moments when neither of them, nor other relatives, were able to find a job. After the lockdown, things improved. Maricela became part of the church, moving beyond her more nominal "evangelical" past. Both Maricela and her husband were able to work enough to pay for the fertility treatment. Finally, Maricela was pregnant.

Suddenly Maricela fell strangely ill. Her body became infected by a parasite unknown to the doctors. The baby was lost, and Maricela was dying, unable to breathe. According to the hospital, her possibilities of survival were very low, even less when she had to be moved to another hospital, where further interventions were available. The church was praying.

Maricela's young brother, Carlos, who would typically hide to avoid the house group when they met, now wanted to join in prayer. He asked us how to make a radical fast. Grace broke through; he met the Lord in a powerful way. All his worldly life was behind. Carlos was baptized, full of joy, in those difficult days. He also began a discipleship. Slowly, Maricela was improving a bit, although still in coma. But God's grace had still more to manifest.

THE GRACE THAT CONFRONTS US

Decades ago, Dietrich Bonhoeffer warned of "cheap grace." He described it as grace where "no contrition is required, still less any real desire to be delivered from sin."[3] Grace comforts, but grace also confronts. The early *Brethren in Christ Confession* excerpted above represents a full spectrum of experience, confronting as well as comforting. The confrontational nature of grace is revelatory, illuminating sin and beckoning us toward a transformed life.

An exchange between Jesus and Peter in Matthew's gospel illustrates the comforting and confrontational nature of grace:

> And they said, "Some say John the Baptist, but others Elijah, and still others Jeremiah or one of the prophets." He said to them, "But who do you say that I am?" Simon Peter answered, "You are the Messiah, the Son of the living God." And Jesus answered him, "Blessed are you, Simon son of Jonah! For flesh and blood has not revealed this to you, but my Father in heaven. And I tell you, you are Peter, and on this rock I will build my church, and the gates of Hades will not prevail against it." (Matthew 16:14–19)

There is something important to observe in the words by Matthew. Clearly, Peter had made a confession of faith: Jesus to him was the Messiah, the Christ. Jesus blesses Peter, but why? Was it for having made a good confession? According to Jesus, Peter was blessed because he had *received* a revelation that did not come from flesh or blood, but from the heavenly Father. It was because of this revelation that Peter was able to proclaim Jesus as the Messiah. Peter not only proclaimed this truth verbally, but also had come to believe it in his heart (Romans 10:9). Peter's experience was not of human origin, but rather had come from God himself. All experience of God comes not from human initiation, but through the initiation of God, who desires to make himself known. Is not this beautiful? God desires for us to know him, and he reveals himself to us toward that end!

Receiving the gift of God is not an addition to the other things already present in our lives. We do not receive Christ simply to bless the whole of our lives, but also to confront that which keeps us from a full life with God. We cannot gain what God desires to give without also losing what God desires to take. This is for our own good and for the sake of Christ in us. No more than a scene later does Peter realize it is one thing to receive revelation, and quite another to reckon with it.

> From that time on, Jesus began to show his disciples that he must go to Jerusalem and undergo great suffering at the hands of the elders and chief priests and scribes, and be killed, and on the third day be raised. And Peter took him aside and began to rebuke him, saying, "God forbid it, Lord! This must never happen to you." But he turned and said to Peter, "Get behind me, Satan! You are a stumbling block to me; for you are setting your mind not on divine things but on human things." (Matthew 16:21–23)

That Jesus would have addressed Peter as "Satan" and referred to him as a "stumbling block" (*skándalon*) must have been a real shock for the disciples. The passage does not give us Peter's reaction. Quite possibly at that moment he did not understand the harshness of Jesus' words. However, during the following days, Peter came face-to-face with what is meant to be a true adversary (*satan*), and a stumbling-block for Jesus.

In contradiction to all his most well-intentioned purposes and his insistent promises (Matthew 26:33, 35), Peter denied his Lord, not just once, but three times! Once Peter realized what he had done, he "wept bitterly" (Matthew 26:75). Without a doubt, Peter found himself to be a sinner.

Sin is not simply a moral failing resulting in a sense of guilt and shame. The biblical word for *sin* in both Hebrew (*khattat*) and Greek (*hamartía*) carries the idea of "missing the mark," much like an arrow that goes off course and misses its target. Sin is not simply a matter of breaking an occasional promise, made in an emotional moment. Sin is failure regarding missing the very purpose of our life, when we have not arrived at what we were created to be, nor accomplished what we wanted with all our strength.

A life in sin is one of pride, living from one's own merits, seeking glory for oneself. In our day, society measures and quantifies the merits of each person, but divides people between those who deserve success, power, and wealth, and those who have lost their way in search of glory. Like Adam and Eve, we want to live by the results of our actions; like Cain and Abel, we want to justify ourselves before God based on what we can offer him. Like the people of Babel, we want to make a great name for ourselves, to be admired by others for our efforts and our technical skills. Pride is one of the great pillars of our culture.

Peter's "bitter weeping" provides a contrast with such pride in our time, when so many are willing to proclaim Jesus as their Savior but refuse to obey him as their true Lord. Perhaps the idea of "lordship" has been emptied of significance and suggests something ancient or religious. What if we were to recognize Jesus as our president, our director, our boss? Perhaps we would be saying something more like what the Jews of the first century understood when they heard the word "Lord."

When we base our lives on our own strengths and merits, we have entered a cycle from which there is no escape. When we want to rid ourselves from sin through our strength, we may achieve some partial success, but we do not eliminate the main problem: living by our own strength. In our day and age, how much counseling, how many addiction cures, how many promises of self-liberation continue to appeal to our own strength, wisdom, and righteousness! They certainly have their place, but the greatest gift these tools can give us is to illuminate our *weakness and need*.

THE GRACE THAT INVITES US

When Jesus rebuked Peter for setting his sights on the things of men, he used an expression that has at times been translated as "Get behind me, Satan!" (Matthew 16:23). Literally, however, the expression used by Jesus was "Get behind me!" (*opíso mou*). It was not meant for Peter to be leading Jesus, but rather Jesus guiding Peter. If Jesus is the Messiah, it is not up to us to tell him what he must do. Peter could not put himself ahead of Jesus; he needed to follow from behind him. Jesus, after rebuking Peter, addressed all of his disciples, saying to them: "If any want to become my followers, let them deny themselves and take up their cross and follow me" (Matthew 16:24).

The words used to rebuke Peter were the same words used to invite him. The rebuke of Jesus is not a rejection of Peter himself, but a confrontation with the part of Peter preventing him from the act of following. Grace's work of confrontation carries with it grace's offering of invitation to follow in a new direction. This is the work of repentance. We really cannot know what sin is until we experience the mercy of God in our sinfulness. Mercy cannot be understood until we realize the ways we have been adversaries of God.

For Peter it was not just the revelation that Jesus was the Messiah. Through a difficult process, the depth of his sin and the immense patience and mercy of God were revealed to Peter. We are invited to follow him as his friends and companions. When Peter realized his deep sin, he wept bitterly, understanding that his following of Jesus was based on his own strength; he had failed in his following of Jesus in a complete and radical way.

THE GRACE THAT ENERGIZES US

Radical Anabaptist obedience is rooted in the experience of the heart, from which arises a holiness that is passionate about *Following Jesus*. After the resurrection, we see Peter twice hurrying up to look for Jesus. First, he runs with the beloved disciple, who arrives first at the empty tomb (John 20:3–6). Later, while fishing in Galilee, Peter hurries to jump into the water to swim towards the shore, where Jesus is. Now he seems to have been the first to arrive! Christian life can be compared to a race (1 Corinthians 9:24–27). But in a race, you can easily be discouraged when you get tired, or you see others run faster than you. Then, you may give up. Here grace makes a defining difference: when you are sure of the prize, you do not stop running; you keep going, whatever it takes. Security about Jesus' love and forgiveness does not make us lazy runners. On the contrary, the certainty of his grace makes us run to Jesus, in the security of the prize of the supreme calling (Philippians 3:12–14).

From the experience of God's grace also comes an authority, promised by Jesus: "I will give you the keys of the kingdom of heaven, and whatever you bind on earth will be bound in heaven, and whatever you loose on earth will be loosed in heaven" (Matthew 16:19).

In Caesarea Philippi, Peter's experience was not yet complete because authority was still a promise. After experiencing his own sin following the death and resurrection of Jesus, Peter was ready to receive power from on high. The keys that Peter received are the keys that all followers of Jesus receive.

The authority that Peter received was not an authority to arbitrarily do whatever he wanted to do. Like Jesus, believers are called to do what we see the Father doing (John 5:19–20). For that, believers need to be filled with the Holy Spirit. When Peter received the Holy Spirit, he was able to proclaim the message of God's grace with no fear whatsoever (Acts 2:14–40; 4:8–12), despite being "uneducated and ordinary" (Acts 4:13). Not only that, but he was also able to pray powerfully for the sick (Acts 3:1–10), to set free the believers from the bonds of tradition, to open the doors of the kingdom to the Gentiles (Acts 10), and much more.

The promise of power to bind and loose is for every disciple, and it is also for the larger community of faith in relationship to one another, *Following Jesus* together. Throughout their history, the BIC never developed complex structures of church authority, and the structures that were developed have always attempted to enable the participation of all believers in the leadership of the church. Further, the BIC have believed in the work of the Holy Spirit *through* each person in the community of faith. As we listen *to* one another we listen *for* the Holy Spirit. Attentiveness to the other is attentiveness to God and God's work among us.

TESTIMONY: SURPRISING GRACE

While Maricela was recovering from her coma, her husband Chepe, who had left his job to stay with her, befriended others in the ICU. There was Yady, a young woman from Colombia. She had suffered from heart failure, which led to irreversible brain damage. Chepe had seen the power of faith in Maricela's case and encouraged Yady's family to believe.

It was not easy. According to the doctors, Yady was gone; "She was no longer there." Only her suffering body was still there. The family had to sign papers allowing the hospital to disconnect Yady from life support and let her body go. Nevertheless, Yady's relatives allowed us to pray for Yady, just like we did whenever we visited Maricela at the hospital.

Carlos also regularly visited his sister Maricela at the hospital. One day, as he was exiting the building, he felt God was telling him to turn around and pray for Yady. He obeyed. It was the first time in his life that he prayed for somebody. Nothing happened. With his first-love faith he just commented: "If God asked me to pray for her, it means that he plans to do something."

A few days later, Yady's family arrived at the hospital to sign the papers to remove life support. The grieving family gathered around Yady's bed to say the last farewell to her body. And suddenly, Yady woke up. She was alive! God's gracious and surprising love brought her back.

ALWAYS NEW GRACE

The experience of the Holy Spirit is an experience of God's love poured out in our hearts (Romans 5:5). The experience of salvation brings with it the filling of the Holy Spirit acting in us with disinterested love, expecting nothing in return. That *agapē* love that characterizes the Christian life is the very same love with which God first loved us, and that we can transmit, as imperfectly as it may be, to others.

The love of Jesus, living in us through the Holy Spirit, compels us to action (2 Corinthians 5:14). The Holy Spirit guides this action, which means followers of Jesus must always be just that: followers. We must maintain a posture of listening for the Holy Spirit, as Israel, guided by cloud and fire.

To the extent that we remain rooted in the experience of God's grace, we will be open to new leadings that the Holy Spirit takes in the church. We see such movements throughout church history, through such renewals as: Protestantism, Anabaptism, Pietism, Holiness movements, evangelistic movements, and charismatic movements. One of the special characteristics of the BIC throughout history has been the willingness to learn from different movements. We do this in community, as we discern together through prayer and relying on the Spirit's leading through the Word of God. How wonderful it is to have an identity that is not set in stone for all time but is forever open to the work of God in history.

TESTIMONY: SHARING OUR EXPERIENCE OF GOD'S LOVE AND GRACE

When Maricela was released from the hospital, she recovered quickly. No wheelchair or other mechanical help was needed. She also visited the first hospital where she was at the beginning of the crisis, to the amazement of the doctors and nurses who thought that she was dead!

Maricela desired no additional fertility treatments when suddenly, like the biblical story of Elizabeth, Maricela was again pregnant. "And this is the sixth month for her who was said to be barren. For nothing will be impossible with God," (Luke 1:36–37). Her brother Carlos, the one who avoided church house groups, is now a fervent evangelist, sharing everywhere he goes about the wonders of God.

GIVING BACK WHAT WE RECEIVED, WHICH IS ALL

The love of God is a sacrificial love (1 Corinthians 13:1–7). Whoever has experienced God's grace and love is ironically someone who has died. It is not just a matter of physical death, as in the case of martyrdom. It is a death that takes place in the baptism of believers who identify with Jesus in his crucifixion (Romans 6:1–4). It is a death to one's own plans, one's own rights, one's life projects, one's own desires. It is not a death that can be imposed on anyone. It is death that is a response to love that has been given and received. Just as Mary poured her most expensive perfume over Jesus (John 12:3), so all those who have experienced God's grace and love are also invited to pour out their own lives, and their plans, out of their love for Jesus.

Our Pietist heritage calls us to the surrender of one's own life, a life valued so deeply by God that it has been purchased by Jesus. Those who lose their life will find it, and they will discover a new, different, renewed life. A life of enjoyment in which everything can be left behind is the very life of Jesus, which we can now live in our simple histories until the end.

A powerful image of this love, and of this holiness, is that of early BIC missionaries, who when they felt called to missions outside their country, packed their humble belongings in a coffin to signify that they had made a permanent decision, and with that radical decision they sailed, *Following Jesus*. They did not consider themselves to be radical at the time; rather, following in simple obedience. They left the old life behind and followed where they felt the Holy Spirit lead.

We are all called to proclaim the good news of the grace of God. But first, we are called to experience it. This experience does not just happen once upon conversion, but in an ongoing way as we follow Jesus throughout the course of our lives. That wonderful grace of God excludes no one. Grace, a singular and concrete gift, cannot just remain as an individual or church privilege. When God called Abraham, he called him to bless all the nations of the earth (Genesis 12:1–3). In the home of Cornelius, a Roman centurion, Peter opened the gates of the kingdom to all nations based on the vision he had received (Acts 10). The experience of God's grace and love, which we have received repeatedly, is destined to be shared with all human beings, in all nations. May the light that shone on the first day of creation keep shining in many hearts, for God's glory and honor.

· · · · · · · · · · · · · · · · · ·

RESPONSE ESSAY
Experiencing God's Love and Grace
▶ *Chinyereugo and Oludamilohun Adeliyi, Dayton, Ohio*

EXPERIENCING A MOVE OF GOD

Less than two hundred years ago, the Church of England established its first mission in Badagry, Lagos, making 1842 the year Christianity was firmly established in Nigeria. Then in 1893 Canadians Walter Gowans and Roland Bingham and American Thomas Kent had a vision to evangelize the sixty million unreached people of sub-Saharan Africa and started what has become one of the largest denominations in Nigeria, Sudan Interior Mission (SIM). These three men came to Nigeria without being "sent." They set out alone because they were unable to interest established mission agencies, most of which said reaching the Sudan was impossible. Gowans and Kent died of malaria in 1894, and Bingham returned to Canada. After two attempts, Bingham sent out a third team that successfully established a base in 1902. Today, a branch of SIM, Evangelical Church Winning All, previously known as the Evangelical Church of West Africa (ECWA), is one of the largest Christian denominations in Nigeria, with about ten million members.

As Christianity spread in Nigeria and throughout Africa, many indigenes began to ask if Christianity was not just a tool of imperialism, where converts gain certain economic and political privileges. It was said the difference between the colonial masters and the missionaries was that the former had guns while the latter had the Bible. Personal experiences of grace were thrown aside as people generally fell into two camps: those who came into the church for the perceived privileges, and those who stayed out because they felt that the church was an extension of colonialism. This yielded a nominal church where there were more pretenders than genuine converts.

However, as Africans began to read the Bible translated into their languages by the missionaries, indigenous revival ensued. Additionally, the arrival of Pentecostalism further shaped the practice of Christianity. From the 1960s to the early 1980s, Christianity in Nigeria experienced its own revival. This revival was also the genesis of a movement that opened up mission work among the majority Muslims in the North and placed Nigeria firmly as one of the leading missionary-sending nations.

These experiences of God have been effective glue binding diverse tribes together in Nigeria, which alone has over five hundred tribes speaking more than two hundred languages. The differences among tribes in Africa are more than their similarities. Multiculturalism succeeds in Christ but breaks down where nominalism prevails. We see this in tribal wars in Africa among some "Christian" tribes; recently, we are seeing it manifest in the United States through the politicization of religion.

In Christ, "There is neither Jew nor Gentile, neither slave nor free, nor is there male and female, for you are all one in Christ Jesus" (Galatians 3:28 NIV). Just as Jesus bonded the disciples from different social and cultural viewpoints, through the Holy Spirit he has bound, and continues to bind, all the tribes together in himself. The point is not that there will be no cultural distinctiveness, but the presence of a Spirit-driven revival subjugates all other feelings under the cross. Once we lose sight of Jesus, our unique differences become magnified and misunderstood, and we resort to fighting in the "flesh."

GRACE-LESS CHURCH

The imposition of religion by the church competes with notions of revival in Nigeria and in many parts of Africa. This imposition is one of the precursors of the "new" syncretism that is prevalent in African Christianity. In many Christianized parts of Africa, like southern Nigeria, it is popular and even fashionable to say that you are a Christian and even "born again," since the custodians of Christian religion reserve respect and honor for those who conform to their brand of Christianity. Here the adage *If you can't beat them, join them* is true. Many now join the church for the same reasons that those in the early parts of Christian growth in Nigeria did—for honor and respect, as well as to fill their bellies.

In the instance described above, the church is not a present reminder of what it means to follow Jesus from behind (Matthew 16:23–24), as mentioned in the essay; rather, it is dictating to Jesus what it wants. In this context, to experience God's grace and love is equated to material and financial blessings. Those who do not enjoy these blessings are either said to be faithless or cursed in some form or the other.

Popular displays of Christianity claim that entrance to the kingdom of God is not by grace through faith but by works through giving. While this may not be directly stated, it is seen in the lives these Christians live and heard through the prayers that come out of their mouths. These prayers are directed to the promoting of self, not to the establishment of the kingdom of God in people's lives and within their communities. While the prosperity message that breeds such a lifestyle is everywhere, it has taken up a life of its own and has modified itself to suit the African audience.

Peter's temptation continues to manifest, just with new terms. This approach is a danger to itself and to others. It is like the lukewarm church described in Revelation. It has no relevance to God or to the society where it is located. In this case, it is like Peter before Jesus rebuked him, wanting the best of Christ, without his suffering, walking before him, not behind.

LOVING OUR ENEMIES

Just as we have *cheap grace*, we also have *cheap love*. Biblical love, however, must first be directed towards God (1 John 4:19). All true love is subjected to God, who is love. While our love cannot be as perfect as God's, disobedience to the One who is love is not a valid way to express the love of God.

The average Nigerian Christian has had their love tested in a different dimension from most Westerners, especially with the advent of Islamic militancy, which has decimated many Christian towns in the North of the country. What are we to do? To seek revenge or not? This has been the question in the heart of the Nigerian Christian for some years now. Our BIC value of *Pursuing Peace* speaks to these questions. The love of God in our hearts does not permit revenge. "Beloved, never avenge yourselves, but leave room for the wrath of God; for it is written, 'Vengeance is mine, I will repay, says the Lord'" (Romans 12:19). To express this kind of love that does not take revenge even for the most heinous sin committed against someone is only possible through the grace of God. It is possible because we are made of a different Spirit and many Christians in Nigeria are living by that Spirit.

• • • • • • • • • • • • • • • • •

RESPONSE ESSAY

Experiencing God's Love and Grace

▶ *Darrell Winger, Oakville, Ontario*

THE EXPERIENCE OF GRACE

The BIC navigate a central way between two extremes in considering a believer's experience of God's love and grace: on one hand, complete reliance on the objective but external traditions and practices of the church, or dependence on one's own subjective, inner experience or understanding. In coming to know the love and grace of God, the Spirit draws a person, and he or she experiences God's free gift of salvation in a way that can be known authentically and personally. However, this experience is not one that is manufactured by each believer's whim or creative choice but inspired and initiated through the prevenient grace of God and received by the individual.

The prevailing cultural trend of the dominance of personal experience determining what is true or valid shapes how the church articulates the nature of experience. However, grace is not something that can be externally coerced by religiously dominant forces, nor is it granted to the believer because of one's inclusion in a particular church tradition or Christian cultural or national context. In our current cultural moment, there is such an overwhelming focus on the individual and the individual's shaping of their own reality.

A true experience of God's grace frees us to submit to Jesus as Lord of our lives and be transformed by him. Spiritual experience in the life of the believer is to further the reign of Jesus in our thinking, words, and actions. We seek to bring glory to Christ rather than draw attention to ourselves. We follow Jesus; we do not follow experience.

THE ROLE OF THE CHURCH

While the inner life of the believer is vital, there is an important and appropriate role for the externally received tradition of the church, too. The prior experience and understanding of Christian believers across the centuries, and in different cultural contexts, gathered up in the teaching, patterns, and practices of the church, provides a tremendously rich well we can draw from to understand and experience God's love and grace. Holding this core value does not mean we are left alone, cut off from previous church history, for each new generation to discern what it means to experience the saving and transforming power of Jesus and follow him as a faithful church. And yet, while patterns and practices are indeed helpful to experiencing and growing in Christ, we must personally and internally experience or know the inner truth or presence of the Spirit. The wealth of previous generations cannot be enjoyed and appropriated unless each believer, and the current community of faith, embraces it.

GOD'S WORK OF GRACE

We receive God's grace in the midst of our sin and brokenness. We need not come to certain levels of knowledge or rise to some level of holiness to receive what God has for us in Christ. The good news is that salvation is a free gift—grace. In the context of our brokenness, we are transformed in an ever-increasing way to reflect Jesus in our lives.

We follow Jesus; he does not follow our commands or our experience. Grace received leads to a life of obedience, a following after Jesus. Our pride and desire to be the one in control of our lives needs to be reordered. Jesus leads us by his Spirit. Our pride tempts us to get the order wrong. The essay rightly cautions us, in light of this cultural moment, that anything, even the best of counseling and care, that appeals to and fosters pride and thinking we are in control, can actually hinder us as it takes the place of Jesus. Love experienced is to be love shared. Our experience of God's love and grace is to be manifest in our love for others. In fact, Jesus' mission for us depends on our experience of his love and sharing of that love.

Further, grace moves us to being people of peace and reconciliation. To know God's forgiveness motivates us to offer forgiveness and see others compassionately rather than as enemies. We are not somehow privileged above other persons or groups of people; all are able to embrace the gift of God's love and grace. This love includes sacrifice—sacrifice of self. Salvation is not about just feeling good, included, or comfortable, but moving beyond our comfort zones to help meet the needs of a hurting world.

THIS VALUE EXPRESSED IN CANADA

Certainly, this has been a core value within the BIC church since its existence in Canada. It has been evident in the life of the church in the past, and in various ways it continues to be a value observed in congregational life across the Canadian church, implicitly and explicitly. For example, it resides at the core of the church's mission: inviting all people to a knowledge and experience of the free gift of salvation in Christ Jesus and the transforming power of the Holy Spirit. It guides the church in its outreach and its focus on discipleship within congregational life and practice. While this may be expressed in diverse ways among the various congregations that comprise the current Canadian church, it is a commonly shared value.

It can be observed in preaching, sermons focusing on God's love and grace, inviting listeners to personally experience God's free gift. That persons would positively respond and apply God's truth on the personal level is a clear goal of the preaching ministry. While the historic "altar call" may no longer be a part of such a response, there continues to be an invitational component or tone to the teaching.

A more experiential focus is often taught, to acknowledge not only head knowledge but a heart knowledge of God's salvation. Teaching will include the invitation to continued spiritual growth, surrender to the Spirit, or experiencing life transformation to reflect the character of Jesus. Admittedly, the language used today differs from that of a few decades ago. Less used is an emphasis on *sanctification* or *holiness*; however, the call to becoming more like Jesus, to going deeper, or to a commitment to spiritual growth expresses the same truth.

Beyond the preaching or teaching ministry, worship services are usually shaped in a way that allows those participating to meaningfully experience God's presence. A practice more common in the past, but still seen, is for members of the church to share their *personal testimony* in some congregational gathering, most often in an evening service or small group setting. This not only affirms the reality of a personal spiritual experience of God's love and grace but strengthens this as a value in the life of the church.

Being rooted in an experience of God's love and grace, we remain open to the new light that God has for us as we are led by the Holy Spirit. Over the last two and a half centuries, the BIC have embraced the leading of the Spirit in its invitation to all persons to experience God's free gift of salvation in Christ Jesus and the transforming power of the Holy Spirit. Though this wonderful truth may now be expressed using new language in various national and cultural contexts in which the BIC exist, it continues to be one of the core values that guides the life and mission of this part of the broader body of Christ.

. . . .
CHAPTER 1

Discussion Questions

1. Why is an experience of grace central to faith in
    Jesus? How do we keep that experience from becom-
    ing something sentimental or self-focused?
2. How is the experience of grace both comforting
    and confronting?
3. What is the difference between proclaiming Jesus as
    Savior and obeying Jesus as Lord?
4. What are stumbling blocks keeping us (the individual
    and the community of faith) from *Experiencing
    God's Love and Grace*?
5. What is the danger of proclaiming the love of God
    without experiencing the love of God?

Believing the Bible

Christina Bosserman

We value the Bible as God's authoritative Word,
study it together, and build our lives on its truth.

INTRODUCTION

When the elders of Israel woke up in their military camp one morning over three thousand years ago, they had to come to terms with their grim situation: four thousand of their own were dead after a gruesome contest with the Philistines. What were they going to tell the grandfathers and grandmothers, sisters and daughters of the fallen? With heavy hearts, the elders asked "Why did God let this happen?" (1 Samuel 4:3). In an instant, the elders manifested the all-too-familiar reflex of anger and broken pride: revenge. They wanted the Philistines to pay, but Israel had been soundly defeated! What power could replace the surviving soldiers' fear with the courage to try again?

Their ancestors were no strangers to this moment. When Joshua asked "Why?" after a defeat at Ai, God helped him gain victory on the second try. And God's answer to Gideon's "Why?" was the defeat of innumerable Midianites with three hundred men and some trumpets. So on that day, when the elders were determining their answer to the Philistines, they knew that their only hope was the power of God. They sent for the ark of the covenant that had led their forefathers to victory at Jericho and Ai, and with great shouts reverberating from Joshua to Gideon to that very moment, they struck fear into the Philistines. But this time, their shouts did not lead to victory; the ark was carried off and they suffered a defeat seven times worse than the one before.

What explains this tragic outcome? A closer look suggests that the elders of Israel saw the ark as a tool to advance their own agenda at best, and an attempt to force God's hand at worst. On the eve of Joshua's victory at Ai, Joshua approached the ark to inquire of the Lord; whereas here, the elders demonstrated no interest in God's words, only his power. The stories of Joshua and Gideon are filled with the phrase "and God said;" yet the phrase does not appear once in 1 Samuel 4. The conclusion is that the elders' fear of failure and desire for revenge had blinded them to God's perspective on their crisis. They put their trust in an object rather than God himself. The ark had become an idol.

A similar scene has played out numerous times over centuries of Christian culture: a Bible verse inscribed on a soldier's weapon, an unopened Bible used as a symbol in the courtroom, or a politician designing a Bible photo op to win the trust of their voters. What does it mean, then, to "believe the Bible"?

VALUING THE BIBLE

A core value of the BIC is *Believing the Bible*. The story of Israel and the Philistines illustrates what this does *not* mean. The BIC do not think the Bible is an object imparting magical powers or political authority. There is nothing innately special about the Bible as an object. The Bible is special because of the testimony of God's people who read it, who believe it contains God's words pointing to the living Word, Jesus, who brings the fullness of God's life to our broken humanity (Ephesians 3:16–19; John 1:1–14).

The Bible has the power to transform us when we read or listen to it in our native language with our hearts and minds eager to understand its message as a message from God. Consider: how does your Bible-reading routine reflect evidence of a lifetime of encounters with the God of the universe? I often ask myself how faithful I would be in reading the Bible if it were not my career. This is certainly not helped by the seismic shift in Western culture towards instant gratification and custom-curated fifteen-second messages that water down the rich experience of reading the Bible's texts over and over again, putting ourselves in its stories, seeing new things every time, and letting it interpret *us* as much as we interpret *it*.

History

What do the BIC mean when we say we *Believe the Bible*?

In 1986 the BIC met to seek an answer to this question. Also happening that year was the writing of the first version of our current *Articles of Faith and Doctrine*.[1] The BIC had a number of confessional statements dating back to 1780, but it was not until 1961, about twenty-five years before the 1986 meeting, that the denomination addressed the Bible at length. Before 1961 the BIC's approach to the Bible was more implicit than explicit; the Bible was assumed authoritative and sufficient for salvation simply because of the Bible's description of itself (Isaiah 55:10–11; John 5:39; 2 Timothy 3:16).

The mid-1900s invited a more explicit approach. This was the height of the BIC's awareness of the "battle for the Bible."[2]

On one side were traditions that held a high view of the Bible, including evangelicals. This side associated the other side with moral permissiveness and questioning the historical credibility of biblical authors and events. Evangelicalism in the 1950s and '60s was a comfortable fit for the BIC, which voiced concerns about the cultural winds they perceived as a threat to biblical authority. Yet quite remarkably, the 1961 and 1986 statements held what we look back on now and affirm as a wise third way. We did not double down on the defensive doctrines of inerrancy or infallibility. Our statements reaffirmed the consistently high view of Scripture inherited from our forebears: the Bible's "full inspiration and absolute authority are emphasized. Its trustworthiness is assumed; it is never even in question. . . this high doctrine of Scripture is maintained without one occurrence of the code words 'inerrancy' and 'infallibility'."[3]

The decision to stay out of the inerrancy debate is not the only notable outcome of the 1986 meeting. A review in *Brethren in Christ History and Life* described an activity that asked participants to brainstorm all the factors they could think of that contribute to a valid interpretation of Scripture. Participants were divided into small groups with a list of forty factors and told to rank the top five. Of the five highest-ranking principles, almost every group out of seventeen had four of those five on their list: 1) The inspiration and illumination of the Spirit, 2) Jesus-centered interpretation and the centrality of Christ's death and resurrection, 3) the New Testament interprets the Old Testament, 4) purity of heart/discipleship, and 5) community consensus.[4] The gift of this meeting was an accessible articulation of standards that had been faithfully stewarded, albeit implicitly, by generations before. These five standards continue to live on in the *Articles* of *Faith and Doctrine, The Brethren in Christ and Biblical Interpretation* study papers (1990), and *10 Guidelines for Reading and Interpreting Scripture* (2013), and have deeply informed the present treatment on our core value *Believing the Bible*.

HOW THE BRETHREN IN CHRIST INTERPRET THE BIBLE

When you pick up a Bible you hold in your hands an object with fixed contents. Whether you have a physical or digital version you will find in each one a piece of literature called *Genesis*. You will not find *The Chronicles of Narnia*. When the BIC say we *value* the Bible, we recognize that the Bible is an object; it is not a philosophy, worldview, or religion. We distinguish between the Bible and interpretations of the Bible. It has a physical presence to it. It came from somewhere and we get no say about what is in it.

The BIC do not depart from Protestant Christianity in defining the Bible as a collection of sixty-six books comprising Old and New Testaments. We depart very little from Catholic Christianity, whose Bible contains an additional seven books that were consulted and preserved like scripture by the first Greek-speaking Christians. Catholic Bibles add *only* those seven books. There are no mystery books that have been snuck into some Bibles and not others. While Catholics and Protestants differ on the precise definition of a "complete" Bible (seventy-three or sixty-six books), the BIC recognize along with the whole of Christian tradition that the Bible is a complete record of God's written revelation. There is no other writing needed for humans to know God's love for the world and God's desire to restore wholeness to God's people, both in this life and in our eternal home.

The challenge of interpretation

In a book about language, the author tells an anecdote of an international student in his class who was majoring in science. He was not a native English speaker, and one day the author used the phrase "solution of my problems" in a lecture. The student went home confused, since his limited English vocabulary, much of it scientific, led him to think of all his problems suspended in liquid, banging up against each other with no way out; it was the opposite of a solution to his problems. The author was illustrating that words spoken or written on a page are meaningless without context and a cultural framework to understand them.

The BIC believe that the Bible contains the words of God. This is a profound statement. God speaks to us! So of course, as spiritually hungry beings, we want to know what God says. And we have been given a very tangible object where we can read every one of those words.[5] But it does not take long to experience the problems with believing that God's words have been recorded in black and white.

Words are risky. They are easily misunderstood. The phrase "sometimes you have to break down a wall to move forward" is a rhetoric to motivate solidarity for one person and a literal call to destruction for another. Contradicting interpretations can happen within hours of the words being spoken. Considering God's words were written over two thousand years ago, how can we possibly know what God *really* meant? For some, this justifies their rejection of the Bible as too lost in ancient culture to carry any objective authority for one's life decisions. This view tends to read the Bible as a collection of good literature that inspires cultural virtues much like *The Lord of the Rings* or *Infinity War* has for recent generations. Actually, this is not bad, as the Bible *is* good literature along the lines of the most profound movies of our time, with a decent track record of inspiring admirable virtues. But as we know, humans have also committed atrocities with *the Bible says*. The problem with this view is that the reader/moviegoer gets to pick and choose what is good in her own eyes. A BIC understanding of the Bible's authority does not allow this posture toward God's words; the posture we see in Eve in Eden, who chooses the serpent's interpretation of God's words to justify her own selfish desires (Genesis 3:1–7), betraying her belief that one's own desires have more authority than God's words.

The BIC affirm that words have meaning, and the meaning of God's words as read in the Bible can be understood. We must be diligent readers of those words because it is true that they come to us through diverse human forms and customs. God inspired authors to put God's words in their own language (Greek and Hebrew). They describe familiar things like human emotion and climate, and unfamiliar things like tribal customs of respecting fathers and blood vengeance. Studying the context of God's words is the *only* way to know what God's words mean. There is no way around it. There are only ways through it.

But the challenge of context is not the only hazard in interpreting the Bible. The story of Adam and Eve illustrates the impact of human sin on interpretation.

Reading through the lenses of desire, fear, and the heart of God

In Genesis 3, Eve's desires led her to choose the serpent's interpretation of God's words, betraying the belief that one's own desires have more authority than God's words. One would think that simply submitting her desires to God's literal words would have led to a different outcome. God's instruction was clear enough, right? "Don't eat from the tree of knowledge." But reading further we learn that God's words are not always to be taken literally. God also said, "In the day that you eat of it you shall die." That day came and went, and they did not die a literal death. The authority of God's words, therefore, was not located in their literal meaning. Indeed, a misplaced literalism may have contributed to Eve's temptation in the first place, but to see this we need to back up to Eve's interaction with the serpent.

In that conversation Eve recited the command: "You shall not eat of the fruit of the tree that is in the middle of the garden, *nor shall you touch it.*" Where did she get the additional command? While more than one answer is possible, a plausible answer is that she got it from Adam.[6] The last time God spoke the command Eve had not been created; only Adam heard it (Genesis 2:17). When she recites the command, she says "God said. . ." but we, the reader, know that God did not say anything about touching the fruit. Either Eve misrepresents God, or she is sincerely reciting what she had been told. Adam's fear of God's words over God himself motivated him to add to those words. Adam thought he could speak for God, which was a rebellion against God's authority equal to Eve's. Rather than pursue the heart of God's words, Adam and Eve succumbed to the emotions of temptation: disordered desire and misplaced fear, and they end up rejecting the very source of their contentment and trust.

What does this have to do with the authority of the Bible? Frequently overheard sentiments about the Bible reflect this struggle between contentment and selfish desire, fear and trust, present in every human heart: "I'm not sure the Bible really teaches ____. The cultural context suggests a different meaning" (desire); "Arguing from cultural context is a justification for disobedience" (fear); "There is a scientific explanation for ____, so the words in the Bible must mean something else" (desire); "If you don't think ____ really happened, it is a slippery slope" (fear).

These convictions divide us when we view the Bible as God's words unattached from God's heart. The truth is, a reader pursuing the heart of God studies the cultural context to truly understand what God's words mean (and don't mean), not to justify her selfish desires. A reader pursuing God's heart accepts the straightforward teachings of the Bible because he fundamentally trusts that God's way is the best way, not because he is afraid of sinning.

We read in a circle: we know the heart of God by reading God's words, but we can't understand God's words without the heart of God. It is admittedly hard, but when we submit to this over a lifetime, God's words will bring fresh insight with new experiences, which will in turn motivate more reading and study to understand God's heart better. The result is a renewed mind (Romans 12:2) and a transformed heart of love towards our neighbor (James 2:8). The authority of God's words is not located in a rational argument for their origin, literalism, or their correspondence to our desires. The authority of God's words is in their function: they teach us, they correct us, and they transform us into humans who reflect God's image in the world (2 Timothy 3:16).

Readers should approach the Bible with a desire to know the heart of God. Practical ways to do this might include:

- Reflect personally on the hazards of sin for interpretation: Is selfish desire tempting you to avoid obedience? Is legalism tempting you to deny your sin? Don't be afraid

to engage God honestly with your answers. God's truth
is matched with abundant grace.

- Before reading the Bible, say a prayer asking God to
  reveal his heart to you.
- Ask God to show you one thing from your study that he
  wants you to put into practice.
- Ask of others questions like "How do you see God's
  heart in this passage?"

Reading through the lens of Jesus

One day a young woman dropped by my office. She and her
mother had exhausted everything they knew to relieve what
I perceived as spiritual warfare. They heard that pastors and
churches might help. As an inexperienced pastor, I was not
exactly sure what to do, but I told her the only power I know
that is capable of freeing her is Jesus (not a pastor), and I
agreed to pray for her. She was not immediately delivered, but
she did make a profession of faith and got baptized. At her
baptism, a number of women shared verses from the Bible
with her, and she admitted she had never read the Bible and it
was very intimidating to her. Yet, as this young woman heard
the Scriptures read to her it was clear that God had taken
the scales from her eyes, and she began interpreting what was
read with the heart of God. An encounter with God transformed her ears to understand the meaning of God's words
without commentaries or classes. This is the same thing that
happened on the road to Emmaus (Luke 24) and in Peter's
dream (Acts 10).

In short, the words of the Bible are not God himself, but
read with purity of heart they lead us to encounter the living
Word of God, Jesus, who has the power to love, forgive, and
transform us into people whose desires are in line with God's

desires. The Bible is best interpreted by God's living Word: the person and work of Jesus as recorded in the New Testament. The BIC *Articles of Faith and Doctrine* affirm that "the person, teaching, and work of Jesus Christ best clarify God's written revelation."[7] The *10 Guidelines* flesh it out more: "We believe that Jesus Christ is the fullest revelation of God and is central to our understanding and interpretation of Scripture," and "The Old Testament should be interpreted through the lens of the New Testament while affirming the integrity of the whole Bible as God's written Word."[8] And in the words of Scripture itself, we believe that "the Word became flesh and lived among us" (John 1:14).

The foundation of a Jesus-centered interpretation is studying the life and teachings of Jesus as recorded in the gospels. A student of God's heart reads the gospels regularly because Jesus is God's heart in the flesh. Then, when reading other parts of the Bible, they look for the same ideas in Jesus' life and teaching. Jesus-centered interpretation can also offer helpful perspectives on difficult passages of other parts of the Bible.

Reading with multiple lenses in the community of faith

The second perspective that helps the everyday reader of the Bible understand what God's words mean is called the community hermeneutic; or, in other words, studying the Bible *together*. It affirms that interpreting God's words on our own is not as reliable as interpreting them with others. This is an extension of reading the Bible with Jesus at the center. The Scriptures say that the church is the "body of Christ." When the church reads the Bible together, they are more likely to hear the heart of God; God's heart is right there among them.

In the early days of the BIC, the community hermeneutic was aimed at a consensus of belief and practice. The church would read and study the Scriptures together and decide "Are women required to wear head coverings? Do we baptize with one or three dunks?" Every two years, leaders from BIC congregations gather at General Assembly to continue this practice of discerning the Holy Spirit's leadership on issues relevant to our own day. Congregations practice this as well, submitting their visions and decisions as a church to prayer and the teaching of Scripture.

The community as a tool for discerning God's heart goes two ways. Individuals come together and make collective decisions about what God wants for their church. The fruit is feeling unified in reliably discerning God's words to them and serving God together. But the community can also help an individual discern if his or her interpretations of the Bible are what God really means. The fruit is the spiritual maturity of the individual. It is the latter that is an important corrective for individualistic cultures like the United States. Individualistic interpretations are all around us: "This interpretation makes sense to me," "You do you," "God told me...," "I agree with Pastor so-and-so." Not to mention that American churchgoers have very fuzzy lines about what community they are accountable to. We may say that we go to "_____ Church," but based on the voices we listen to in a week, how many of us actually go to YouTube Church? Unfortunately, YouTube is far more likely to show us messages we want to hear than hold us accountable to correct interpretations of Scripture.

I wonder what would have happened if Adam and Eve had practiced a community hermeneutic to correctly understand God's command? Adam was with Eve when she ate the fruit (Genesis 3:6–7). I suggested earlier that Eve and Adam exhibited the emotions of temptation: desire and fear. Adam decided that to ensure obedience he needed to add to God's command words that were not there. His ability to support Eve's walk with God was diminished by taking authority for himself that belonged to God. How often in a well-meaning desire to protect loved ones from the consequences of sin do we pass off as biblical rules that are expansions of God's words? The point is not to give permission to sin; the point is that your brothers and sisters do not need legalistic additions to God's words to become competent interpreters of the Bible. They have their own gifts, their own sin, their own accountability before God, and have to wrestle with God's *actual* words for themselves.

What if, instead of adding to God's words, Adam had repeated God's actual words and engaged her in conversation? "Eve. . . this is what the command sounded like when I heard it. . . . God didn't say anything about touching it but I think we shouldn't because I care very much that we honor God. . . . Why do you think you are attracted to the serpent's words? . . . Let's go talk to God about what 'wise' means." As for Eve, her desires made the serpent's interpretation that validated them sound more convincing. But did it have to end that way? Sometimes all it takes is a wise word from a brother or sister to recognize our desires and see our error. What if in that moment Eve had asked for Adam's input, or Adam had spoken up out of care for Eve's spiritual welfare? Perhaps Eve could have been enlightened to her selfish desire. We aren't told why Adam's silence was not overcome with love for Eve, only that he remained silent. In short, God did not need Adam and Eve to build a hedge by adding to his words. He gave them each other as that hedge. Consider a few practical applications of this idea:

1. It is far too easy to find Christians who will tell us what we want to hear, so make a commitment to a

faith family whether that is through membership or a commitment of the heart. Then you can't just up and leave when you hear something you don't like.

2. Pursue diverse voices. Humans tend to gravitate towards people like themselves. Read diverse authors, watch cross-cultural movies and documentaries, and be curious about those who are different than you.

3. You have great value to your church. If a person thinks that the most academic ones or most spiritual ones are better at understanding what God means by his words, and that forces a person to stay quiet, then important perspectives will be lost.

4. Pursue a setting to talk about the Bible. Some easily speak up in large group settings. A smaller group should be safe, but not necessarily comfortable; the transforming authority of the Bible demands discomfort.

5. Foster the skill of asking clarifying questions. It is illuminating to get to the motivation behind an individual's interpretation.

And lastly, while an individual may say at some point, "God told me. . . ," unless God confirms the word through the Holy Spirit in the hearts of others in the community of believers, we respond reluctantly.[9]

Putting what we read into practice
Believing the Bible means three primary things:

1. We read and study God's words with a sincere desire to know what they mean so we can be led to an encounter with the living Word.

2. The presence of the living God among "two or three gathered" is God's design for a protective hedge against misunderstanding his words (Matthew 18:20).

3. We put God's words into practice with the help and accountability of our Christian brothers and sisters.

There is no one method for finding the significance of God's words for daily life. Some rely heavily on the illumination of the Holy Spirit both in their reading and in application. Others use a more tangible approach, like observing the life setting of a biblical text and identifying themes or principles that can be applied to an equivalent setting in the believer's life. The former can become too subjective without the accountability of the community. Likewise, the latter can become legalistic when one's conclusion is followed rigidly even when the setting has changed. The main thing is that we should do what we read: "The shape of obedience has changed greatly [over the years]. That is good; had the shape not changed we would no longer be obedient to the principles for living that God gives us. At the same time, we face the strong danger of relinquishing obedience. God does not change, nor does his Word. We commit ourselves also not to change in our commitment to follow Christ in life and death."[10]

. . . .

RESPONSE ESSAY

Believing the Bible

▶ *Dave Downey, Dillsburg, Pennsylvania*

ALIGNING BELIEF AND PRACTICE

The author consistently circles back to a critical question: What does it actually mean to *believe the Bible*? It is easy for Christian communities to claim a high view of the Bible, but how do we know if it is actually true?

I am reminded of a recent conversation I had with my father-in-law, who serves as an elder at a church in the Chicago area. As they work to hire a new senior pastor, the search firm requested that each staff and elder complete a survey that included reflections on the strengths and weaknesses of the community. A high view of the Bible surfaced as a consistent strength. However, in a recent meeting, one of the elders voiced passionate disagreement. He posed questions like: How do we have a high view of the Bible when our staff team is in constant tension and cannot get along? How can we confidently make this claim when the fruits of the Spirit are lacking in our community? What a great set of questions!

POSTURE OF OBEDIENCE

The BIC possess a high view of the Bible as we emphasize doing what it says. *Believing the Bible* means a commitment to live the Bible in our context. Theology matters, but not all theology is good theology. The goodness of our theology is reflected through lived habits and practices. As BIC, the Bible is our guide to faith and life, just as it was for Jesus. Jesus was anchored in the Scriptures. Because the most prominent way we learn about Jesus is in the Bible, then we are committed to the Scriptures and recognize their inspiration and authority. The essay prompts us towards a posture of obedience to the Bible by emphasizing putting God's words into practice.

Too often, we use incomplete metrics for measuring belief in the Bible that marginalize an emphasis on obedience. This can be illustrated in two ways:

- A quantitative approach: whoever opens their Bible the most wins! While putting in the time to read and learn the Bible is a critical practice for any follower of Jesus, focusing on how much we read can lead to missing the forest for the trees. Checking off the devotional box of the daily checklist matters little if reading the Bible is not followed by obedience.

- A doctrinal approach: reading the Bible to find the "right" doctrinal position. As the essay illustrates, this approach can encourage overly politicized and self-serving battles for the Bible that divide the people of God. A posture of obedience is critical here. Is it more important to check the right box on a doctrinal questionnaire about the Bible or to obey what it says?

If we are not careful, our confident declarations of possessing a high view of the Bible may represent hermeneutical narcissism, where we are in love with our own interpretations and knowledge of the Bible rather than submitting ourselves to the scriptures that point us to Jesus. I resonate with the essay's insight that we should allow the Bible to interpret us, rather than only seeking to interpret the Bible.

READING SCRIPTURE IN THE LOCAL CONGREGATION

As a pastor, I constantly wrestle with what it means to gather a community around scripture with a posture of obedience.

This is a challenge when many in and outside of the church do not trust or hold the Bible in high regard. For many, the Bible is actually a barrier to faith! It may be because of the difficult passages in the Bible, verses they have heard out of context, or the tone of Christian dialogue on social media.

Recently, I had a couple reach out in search of a pastoral conversation; they were in full-blown "deconstruction" mode. Raised in a highly fundamentalist context, they were indoctrinated into a long list of beliefs that were essential to be a legitimate, "Bible-believing" Christians. Unless you took the whole bundle—literal six-day creation and all—you were on the slippery slope to a wishy-washy progressivism that was destined to abandon the authority of Scripture. This way of faith and theology no longer worked for this couple. Disoriented, they were trying to put some pieces back together and discover their own views of the Bible.

I love these conversations because they are courageous and honest. In navigating conversations like these I am reminded of several convictions we must keep central in *Believing the Bible* today:

- We should be hesitant about dogmatically claiming an absolutist "biblical view" on an issue. Too often this leads to self-righteousness and over-confidence. As we grow in knowledge of the Bible, we realize all that we do not know. Hermeneutics is not an easy task. The church past and present is littered with examples of incomplete or wrong interpretations. In my own theological journey, I have changed my view or had convictions reshaped significantly. We should engage a life-long pursuit of a faithful reading of the Bible, not a quick process of for-ever landing on the right positions. In doing so, we will increase space in our congregations for those who doubt or question, and encourage a spirit of humility.

- We must relentlessly pursue a Jesus-centered hermeneutic. Consequently, we cannot engage a flat reading of the Bible in which each verse carries equal weight. The life of Jesus as revealed in the gospels takes center stage and pulls us into the rest of the story.
- The Bible is a gift. Sometimes this is forgotten in our intense academic pursuits or our complacent movement away from the authority of Scripture. As we read and teach the Bible, we should do so with gratitude, recognizing that we follow a God who speaks to us.

• • • • • • • • • • • • • • • • • •

RESPONSE ESSAY
Believing the Bible

▶ *Maria Perdomo, Miami, Florida*

We cannot know God if we do not have the revelation of Scripture through the guidance and direction of the Holy Spirit. The Scriptures are God's message for our lives, expressing and declaring God as creator and preserver of all things. The most wonderful revelation was made through his Son Jesus Christ, and the Scriptures are those that testify about him.

I have understood that a minister has no more powerful tool than the Word of God. Its truth has transforming power to change human lives. While we have in our library reference books, Bible dictionaries, concordances, inspirational and historic Christian books, all of which can be of great use, it is only the Bible that can transform the heart of humanity. When the Holy Spirit takes that word and makes it a revealed and powerful word, *rhema* (Hebrew for *voice*) in a heart, it is like a hammer that breaks the rock (Jeremiah 23:29), a lamp that guides us (Psalm 119:105), and a sword that penetrates to the ends of our being transforming our lives. As Hebrews 4:12 says: "Indeed, the word of God is living and active, sharper than any two-edged sword, piercing until it divides soul from spirit, joints from marrow; it is able to judge the thoughts and intentions of the heart."

Christians are called to read and obey God's Word and this truth of God sets us free and sanctifies us. The triune God works in the purity, transformation, and sanctification of the heart of those who believe in Christ, and we see how the third person of the Trinity, the Holy Spirit, makes us fruitful in our lives and to be effective disciples.

I am committed to preaching God's Word because it brings change in all our actions, involving renewal and transformation of our thoughts and behaviors (Romans 12:2). Through the Word we grow to the stature of the perfect man, Jesus, and in our faith, for faith comes by hearing and hearing by the word of God (Romans 10:17). In the Bible I have also found powerful promises declaring that God is present in our daily lives and in all human events and situations.

The Bible should be for all believers the rule of Christian faith and practice. The church and its leaders must preach and teach the Word and establish the praxis of its content in our daily lives. The Word is to be lived and put into practice, not just read and heard. It is ". . . useful for teaching, for reproof, for correction, and for training in righteousness, so that everyone who belongs to God may be proficient, equipped for every good work," as Paul tells us in 2 Timothy 3:16–17. The Word of God works in the believer in practical and powerful ways bringing about transformation.

CENTERED ON JESUS

God has revealed himself to us in different ways and forms. However, the most powerful revelation of all is the living word, the incarnate word—Jesus Christ, the word of God in action. Jesus is the Word made flesh, who manifested his glory among us (John 1:1–14). The centrality of Christ, his death and resurrection, are the backbone of Scripture and of our faith. For the BIC, the centrality of Jesus is fundamental to what it means for us to *believe the Bible*.

Jesus himself said, "Search the scriptures because you think that in them you have eternal life; and it is they that testify on my behalf" (John 5:39). In the Bible, we learn of Jesus' mission and redemptive work on the cross to redeem humankind

(Isaiah 61:1–3). God's most wonderful revelation was made through his Son Jesus Christ, and the Scriptures are those that testify about him. His works, teaching, preaching, miracles, healings, principles of the Kingdom of God, character and life, saving work, are fully understood through the study of the Bible and reveal the heart of God.

INTERPRETATION

The Scriptures are God's message to us, written by people in different times, contexts, and languages. However, God does not cancel the personality, culture, context, education, or language when he transmitted his message to humanity through the Word.

The Old Testament points to the person of Jesus Christ as God's ultimate revelation to man. In the New Testament, Jesus Christ demonstrated through his person, acts, preaching, and teaching his mission as Savior of the world. He fulfills the Scriptures and God's promises for God's people, Israel, and for all humanity. Jesus Christ is the word of God in action. "The Word became flesh and lived among us," (John 1:14).

Community consensus is important, as emphasized in the essay. This is very relevant because in our time we see that the most common errors are the private, individual, and exclusive interpretation of persons or entities. There are also those who confuse the differences between historicist, symbolic, doctrinal, and literal interpretations. We have seen how many seek to accommodate the new doctrinal and cultural winds of our time, being permissive with sin, entering religious and doctrinal syncretism, or undermining biblical authority. A community consensus helps ensure a more faithful reading of the Bible.

Lastly, we need the illumination and inspiration of the Holy Spirit as we read the Bible. The Holy Spirit guides to all truth. As John 17:17 tells us: "Sanctify them in the truth; your word is truth." It is not that it contains partial truth, but it is the truth of God revealed in its entirety. The Holy Spirit has inspired and continues to reveal and interpret the Scriptures. Although we attempt to understand and interpret the Scriptures, using different methodologies and ways to understand the eternal truths of God, it is only the Holy Spirit, the most excellent teacher, who reveals the hidden treasures and precious truths of the word of God to us.

. . . .
CHAPTER 2

Discussion Questions

1. In what ways is it possible for the Bible to be an idol?
2. What is your practice of reading the Bible? Was there ever a time that reading the Bible was a confusing or intimidating experience? What helped you get more comfortable?
3. What emotion of temptation resonates with you more: desire or fear? Has it affected how you read the Bible?
4. What do you think about the idea that God gave us each other as a protective "hedge" against misunderstanding the Bible?
5. What primary thoughts or feelings do you have when you think about sharing your interpretations of the Bible with others? What are some ways an individual believer or your church can practice the community hermeneutic?

Worshiping God

Alan Claassen Thrush

We value heartfelt worship that is God-honoring,
Spirit-directed, and life-changing.

INTRODUCTION

Several years ago, I visited the Grand Canyon with a plan to watch the sunset from a designated canyon overlook. In my mind, I had prepared for a quiet moment of reverent worship, soaking in the majesty of God's creation as the setting sun threw spectacular colors across the sky and canyon walls. I realized the flaw in my plan, however, when I arrived in the filled-to-the-brim parking lot. The small outcrop overlook could barely contain the throngs of other tourists as we jostled and elbowed for the best views. As I shuffled from one spot to the next, a new thought occurred to me: the natural landscape, while awe-inspiring, was *not* the most spectacular part of God's creation right around me. Instead, Genesis 1:26–27 came to mind, which describes the crown jewel of God's creation: it wasn't the land or the sky, but the *people*. I started paying attention to the men and women around me. They came from all over the world, speaking many languages and reflecting many cultures. Remarkably, *we* reflected God's image in a way that outshone the setting sun.

This memory from the Grand Canyon came back to me several years later when I participated in a multicultural worship experience. The gathering brought Christians together from many countries, with many languages, cultures, and church traditions represented. The difference was that we gathered not to watch a sunset, but to worship the One who created it. We had several gatherings, and each time the worship planners did a masterful job incorporating elements from many languages and styles. Everyone felt a little uncomfortable singing in a language or style not our own, and at the same time we were grateful to join brothers and sisters in worship of the Creator God.

The BIC identify *Worshiping God* as one of the core values that shape Christian discipleship. As the BIC approach 250 years of being a community of disciples, we reflect anew on how these values shape us together. The biblical and theological foundations of worship remain the same from generation to generation; likewise, so is the temptation for each generation of Jesus followers to be shaped by everything *but* God. This essay invites us to recommit ourselves to lives and communities shaped by God-honoring and Spirit-guided worship.

MEANING AND CONTEXTS OF WORSHIP

So what *is* worship? Worship refers to the habits and rituals that we perform for the things we love.[1] It is not an inherently *religious* activity. As one writer put it, "In the day-to-day trenches of adult life. . . there is no such thing as not worshiping. Everybody worships. The only choice we get is what to worship."[2] Martin Luther said, "Whatever your heart clings to and confides in, that is really your god."[3] As humans, we love, and we develop habits and rituals around those things we love—that is worship. Think about our contemporary habits with our smart devices and social media. Algorithms track the things our hearts cling to via our clicks, and then present us with more of the same information that will generate more clicks. The clicks become habits that lead us into virtual echo chambers that reaffirm limited versions of reality—"*This is the way the world* really *is.*" In short order, our smart devices shape our habits and our loves.

Scripture reveals that humans constantly love the wrong things—money, power, prestige, sex, influence, and more. All these things become our gods, whether we are conscious of it or not, and none of these gods give life. The Scriptures also reveal our forgetful human natures: even when we know that these other things cannot give life, we forget and keep returning to them. We forget the divine order—that we are dependent on God; we forget how God has acted in the past, and we doubt that God will act in the present or future.

The Bible offers an alternative: when we make God the center of our love and orient our lives around Jesus, only then do we find and experience true life. *Christian* worship, therefore, is all about God as the source and object of our love. Worship is both our relational posture towards God as the one who gives us ultimate meaning and value,[4] and the habits and rituals that shape and orient that relationship.[5] Worship is the act of "recalibrating our hearts."[6] In worship we remind ourselves of who God is, what God has done, and what God will do in our lives and in the world.[7] We gather around the Scriptures to tell and retell God's story. We listen for the Holy Spirit speaking in community. And we allow the transforming work of Jesus—demonstrated through his sacrificial life, death and resurrection—to give us imagination to trust that God will be faithful as he was in the past.

RECALIBRATION

Given the constant messages and voices clamoring for our allegiance and worship, recalibration of our hearts and minds is critical for healthy Christian discipleship. Everything related to our jobs, family, marriages, friendships, neighborhood engagement, etc., should reflect allegiance to God and, therefore, require recalibration (Colossians 3:23). The BIC are committed to forming disciples whose whole lives are oriented towards Jesus as King, and we endorse individual worship practices like Scripture study, music, art, outdoor activities, prayer, fasting, service, generosity, etc. In addition, we understand that worship is more than individual life-orientation. God does not just call individuals into relationship with him, he calls individuals into relationship *together* to have relationship with him. Worship, therefore, is also "a meeting between God and his people."[8] As the BIC, we value the recalibration of our community's hearts and imaginations to be loyal to God's story.

God wants to be known

From the earliest stories of the Bible, we find a God who wants to be known by his creation. In Genesis 1, God's creative actions culminate in the formation of humanity (Genesis 1:26–27). God walks with them and interacts with them in a close relationship (Genesis 3:8). Things quickly went wrong (Genesis 3), but God never gave up his image-bearers. The Bible shows God pursuing humans because he wants us to know and trust him. God revealed himself to Moses at the burning bush (Exodus 3); he showed himself to the people of Israel through the signs and wonders of the Exodus (verses 12–14, 19); he compared himself to a husband pursuing his unfaithful wife through the prophet Hosea. God relentlessly pursues us, and he promises that when we pursue him, he can be found (Jeremiah 29:13).

Even though the relationship with God changed after sin entered creation, God remained committed to a relationship with humans. Since it is not possible for humans to enter into God's presence without protection or consequence, God therefore established boundaries around the spaces—the tabernacle and temple—within which his people could experience his presence (Exodus 25–28). God worked with these restrictions for centuries, yet God's desire was always to return the creation to an Eden-like state, where God could walk with humans without fear or consequence. Jesus began removing the barriers between us and God, as evidenced with the tearing of the curtain separating the profane and the holy in the temple, torn in two at his death (Matthew 27:51), giving us access to a direct relationship with God. Jesus then sent the Holy Spirit to guide and empower the church in his absence (John 14:15–21).

Both constant and occasional

When we affirm that every aspect of life gives glory to God, in an important sense our lives become acts of worship. Paul affirmed that the Holy Spirit renews the minds of those who follow Jesus, and such transformed thinking and behavior are spiritual acts of worship (Romans 12:1–2). Paul also encourages us that the Holy Spirit dwells in our bodies as temples—individual points of intersection between heaven and earth (1 Corinthians 6). At the same time, a constant life of worship cannot be maintained without participation in regular episodes of worship. These episodes have looked different throughout history. For the ancient Israelites, these involved worship in the temple and regular feasts and festivals. The worship episodes of the early church involved small home gatherings with prayers, singing, and Scripture (Ephesians 5:18–19). The BIC in the United States gather for worship in buildings of various sizes, on different days and in different languages and styles.

Both planned and spontaneous

God invited God's people into relationship through worship by providing structure and guidelines. In the Old Testament, the structure functioned to protect the sinful people from God's holiness while at the same time allowing them to draw near to God. In the New Testament, the guidelines helped the early church to interact together in orderly and respectful ways (1 Corinthians 11:17; 1 Corinthians 14). God invites us to relate to God intentionally, with thought and planning that help us to prepare to experience the fullness of God and learn respectfully together as a community.

At the same time, we recognize that the Holy Spirit moves in ways that our plans do not anticipate. Acts 2 tells the story of the early church receiving the Holy Spirit. The disciples and other Jesus followers had gathered in a room for worship and prayer, when suddenly something entirely unexpected happened: tongues of fire rested on the head of each person, a sound like a mighty wind rushed through the room and each person began sharing the good news of Jesus in other languages. The Holy Spirit moves according to its own wisdom and is not a thing we can control. As such, sometimes the Spirit leads us into spontaneous expressions of worship.

THE STRUCTURE OF OUR WORSHIP

In Deuteronomy 6, God instructed his people to tell and retell God's story to the next generations. God wanted them to be intentional, knowing that in the absence of a plan, the people would forget what God had done (Deuteronomy 6:12). We are no less forgetful today than the people of Israel—and perhaps have even more distractions that divert our attention. Thankfully, we do not have to reinvent the wheel when it comes to recalibrating our hearts towards God. We build on the wisdom and experience of centuries of other believers.

Four key elements

Throughout history, Christians of various traditions have developed resources to tell God's story and recalibrate hearts in a coherent way. One of the most common resources is a simple four-part structure to a worship service: 1) Gathering, 2) Word, 3) Response/Table, and 4) Sending.[9] These four elements provide a balanced plan to ensure that the community experiences the full range of God's story in the course of a worship service. The beauty of this simple structure is that it is adaptable for any style and cultural context. The BIC, as part of an informal, low-church tradition, has tended to not use formalized and unified plans for worship across congregations. Over its nearly 250-year history, the BIC have allowed for great freedom from community to community when it comes to the form, style, and shape of each worship event. A weakness of this freedom, however, is that local communities may end up with isolated worship practices or in worship ruts that only reflect a small portion of God's story in Scripture. This four-part structure can help worship planners and leaders avoid the ruts and instead plan a more complete heart-recalibration experience.

Honest, heart-felt communication

The Psalms offer templates for how to engage with God in our worship experiences. They are the rich and nuanced prayers of generations of faithful people, honest, raw, and filled with emotion. Sometimes the prayers are joy-filled and exalt God's majesty. At times they overflow with sadness and grief. Still others express anger and anguish over injustice and God's seeming silence in the face of evil. God welcomed and invited all the emotions that God's people brought to their worship. The Psalms provide examples of how we can bring our own emotions and feelings to God in worship. God wants honest communication that comes from our hearts. God wants to know when we feel joy and when we feel crushed and defeated. God welcomes our hopes, fears, doubts, and anger into worship because God wants us to be honest with him. God knows things are not okay all the time, and God wants us to bring everything in our hearts to him in worship.

PRINCIPLES FOR WORSHIP IN THE TWENTY-FIRST CENTURY

BIC communities look different and face new challenges in the twenty-first century than they did even a generation ago. For the first two centuries, BIC churches were filled with people from Swiss and German ethnic heritage, and with many based in rural, agricultural communities. Today, BIC churches in the United States are found in rural, suburban, and urban contexts, with members from many cultural backgrounds and languages. Technological innovation has made available a world of resources and connections that did not exist in previous generations. We now have instant connections with people in other parts of the country and world. As BIC, we must think wisely and creatively about how our worship engages the resources around us so that we form men and women of faith and equip one another to be ministers of the gospel wherever we go. Ultimately, worship is not about the songs we sing or the feelings we experience in worship gatherings. It is instead about practicing something as individuals and as a community that points us to God and reminds us of our calling as followers of Jesus.

Finding shared identity

The presence of psalms in scripture represents an example of how shared worship resources create a shared identity in a community over time. People that prayed the Psalms were shaped and molded by the prayers as they offered language that helped God's people express a full range of emotions to God. Likewise, throughout Christian history, groups of Jesus followers have developed resources that they have shared and that have shaped them in a particular way. A technical implication of finding a shared identity relates to our worship resources. Previous generations of the BIC used the hymnal as a unifying worship resource. For example, a BIC church in California in 1930 could expect that BIC brothers and sisters in Ohio would sing similar songs in worship gatherings.[10] This was important in times when many people did not have access to recorded music. The only way to share songs and music was to print the lyrics and music in books—and teach people how to read music so that communities could join in song.

If we are not shaped by a common set of worship resources—including music and the arts—what shapes us as BIC communities of believers? If there are no thoughtful BIC frameworks for selecting songs and worship resources, churches risk sharing fewer and fewer things in common. If BIC churches do not share worship resources (including, but not limited to songs), what are the things that churches *do* together that shape people in similar ways? Likely the worship resources of the past—particularly hymnals—are not adequate to respond to the contemporary reality. This reflection is an invitation for BIC individuals and communities to dedicate creative energies towards sharing worship resources that uniquely reflect BIC core values and that help shape us in similar ways.

A theological implication for finding a shared identity relates to the language we use in worship. As mentioned above, the BIC care about forming individuals *and* communities in the way of Jesus. A common modern tendency is to see worship gatherings as groups of individuals experiencing God.

Connecting with the global body of Christ

Worship experiences connect deeply with our emotions, our understanding of God and our cultural contexts. The worship resources—particularly music—present when a person comes to faith in Christ tend to be the resources and styles that they most resonate with throughout their lifetime. In addition, each of us grows up in families or neighborhoods with their unique musical and artistic styles that bring comfort and joy. This is natural and good—we want people to experience heart-felt communication with God that emerges from our cultural contexts.[11] God also makes himself known in every time, place, and culture. So we celebrate the fact that God enters into our own lives and cultural contexts, and that we can communicate to God in styles and expressions that come from our hearts.

At the same time, it is important to remember that God is not only the God of our own cultural subgroup; God is also God of the whole world. Our understanding of God can expand when we embrace worship resources from outside our communities, traditions, and cultures. Fortunately, technology gives us easy access to learn from Christian brothers and sisters—including BIC communities—in different places. Worship experiences are ultimately about us learning to embrace

God's big, global story of redemption. BIC churches can grow in wisdom, maturity, and depth of insight when we commit to expanding our worship horizons and embrace practices that are not our "preferred" style.

Extending hospitality

The practice of Christian worship makes sense for Jesus followers who want to be shaped by God's story in Scripture. Christians understand the importance of setting aside regular time to gather around the Bible, to sing and pray together, and to share in community life. These practices remain strange, however, for those who have not yet chosen to follow Jesus. As the United States increasingly becomes a post-Christian society, where the average citizen attends a religious gathering with less frequency, it is important that we remember how strange a Christian worship gathering may seem to people with little faith background.

The early church regularly received encouragement to practice hospitality as part of their Christian discipleship (1 Timothy 5:10; Hebrews 13:2). One component of hospitality is welcoming people into our space and helping them feel a sense of belonging.

When it comes to our times of worship, BIC churches do well to remember that in any given event, a new person might be present who has no idea what is going on or why certain events take place. Practicing hospitality in worship does not mean trying to offer visitors what they want. Rather, hospitality means explaining the elements and rationale of worship in simple terms, creating spaces in which people feel welcome, and inviting participation as people feel comfortable. In fact, hospitality in worship can prove useful even for Christians who have participated for many years; it is easier than we may think to get comfortable in worship routines and forget the "why" behind actions.

Encouraging active participation

God invites every Christian into relationship through a Christian community. Worship events provide opportunities for each person to hear from God and to respond with praise, gratitude, lament, and service. Worship emanates from us collectively as an expression of the community's commitment to follow Jesus. As such, worship events prove more effective and transformative when the community is invited and expected to participate.

This does not mean that every person must have the same level of participation, or that there is no place for individual elements in worship. Individuals with certain gifts and talents can be invited to share their gifts with the community in ways that encourage the group; for instance, when a soloist sings the Lord's Prayer, or a poet shares a poem. We should be cautious, however, of the tendency to treat worship experiences like performances—where one group of people produces worship while another group of people consumes it. This is a particular temptation for churches that expect a certain level of skill or professionalism at a worship event. Professional concert experiences with professional musicians *can* be worship, but they can also quickly become concerts.

Christian discipleship also involves investing in the next generation of Jesus followers, teaching and training them in the story of God's saving work. Much of this training and teaching happens in the worship services of the gathered community. It is the collective space where we people of all ages gather around God's Word and recount the stories of who God is and what God has done. Children and youth learn about the habits of faith and worship when they participate with adult believers in the activities of worship. Recent research confirms what the scripture writers also knew: the most important factors that influence whether children and youth will remain a part of the Christian community are whether the children and youth feel connected to the adults in their faith communities.[12] As such, the BIC want to include people at all ages and stages of faith in worship gatherings—from the youngest to the oldest, from the least to the most experienced.

Nurturing skill and heart

Skill and heart represent two important considerations for BIC worship in the twenty-first century.[13] Since worship is the community's engagement with God and God's story, it creates space for us to hear from God and be transformed as a community. Meaningful worship requires good leadership to help with the planning and execution of the various elements. This is especially true for the musical, technological, and artistic elements of a worship event. To that end, Christian communities need to encourage excellence in skill so that worship events flow smoothly and have integrity and coherence.

God welcomes our skills and talents to benefit the church community, and God is concerned about our hearts (1 Samuel 16:7). We can learn from David on this point, as the psalmist commends him for leading with both skillful hands and integrity of heart (Psalm 78:72). Local BIC leaders should ensure that those tasked with leading the community in worship attend to both skill *and* heart. It does not mean that those who lead must be perfect. But BIC leaders should exercise caution when inviting only highly-skilled people to lead while overlooking the heart. The lack of attention to the heart can lead to obstacles for the community of believers to truly participate in the worship experience.

Another of the BIC core values is *Believing the Bible*. We do this by allowing the Scripture to shape us as we read and listen to it together in worship. BIC communities can ensure that Scripture plays a leading role in worship gatherings by following Scripture reading plans that cover a large portion of Scripture over the course of several years.

USING SYMBOLS AND PRACTICES

The BIC of the twenty-first century reflect the diversity of language, culture, style and even theological emphasis: we are people shaped by Anabaptist, Pietist, Wesleyan, and Evangelical traditions. We are very different, and the worship gatherings of BIC communities will reflect this diversity. But we share a commitment to the same Lord: to have our hearts calibrated towards Jesus and to be his disciples (Ephesians 4:4–6).

Two worship ordinances—baptism and the Lord's Supper—unite us in common action. Baptism is the public act affirming faith in Jesus. The symbolic immersion into water three times—in the name of the Father, Son and Holy Spirit—demonstrates "submission to Jesus Christ and identification with his death and resurrection. We expect baptized believers to commit themselves to the membership covenant, thereby affirming their loyalty to the church."[14] The Lord's Supper, or communion, is the symbolic meal that reminds us of Jesus' saving actions through his body on the cross. It also unites us "with believers of all times and places. We are to examine ourselves in the light of Scripture before approaching the Lord's Table. Reconciliation with God and with brothers and sisters in Christ is an essential preparation for participation."[15]

The BIC also identify five practices in the New Testament—actions that, while not prescriptive, have high recalibration potential for Jesus followers: 1) footwashing; 2) a Christian marriage ceremony; 3) dedication of children; 4) prayer for healing and deliverance; and 5) a Christian funeral. These occasional practices happen in the context of worship events. They can reflect the styles and subcultures of a local BIC church, but they unite us in their symbolic actions to shape the community.

While a largely unfamiliar practice in twenty-first century, footwashing was common in the ancient world and practiced upon entering a home. John 13 describes how Jesus washed his disciples' feet during their final Passover meal, demonstrating servanthood and sacrifice and instructing them to do the same. Historically, the BIC have practiced footwashing as part of Holy Week, on the Thursday before Easter (Maundy Thursday). A fellowship meal, called a love feast, sometimes opens the community time. In the absence of a common meal, a time of singing and scripture may open the footwashing service. Men and women separate into different spaces and sit in circles. An individual wraps a towel around the waist, takes a basin of water and kneels before a seated brother or sister. The kneeling person scoops water onto one foot, dries it with a towel, then repeats the process with the other foot. Sometimes the kneeling person shares an encouraging word or offers a prayer or scripture for their brother or sister. The two then stand and embrace with a word of blessing. The person whose feet have just been washed then receives the towel and proceeds to wash the feet of the next person. People around the circle can lead in songs, prayer, or scripture passages. After everyone has washed the feet of a neighbor and had their feet washed, the men and women reunite and celebrate the Lord's Supper together.

Washing one another's feet offers a powerful and tangible expression of servanthood and humility and helps recalibrate our hearts. The act of kneeling before a brother or sister reminds us that we are called to humble ourselves and serve one another. The act of allowing our feet to be washed reminds us that Jesus invites us to submit to one another (Ephesians 5:21). Humility and service are so central, in fact, that the symbols of footwashing (the basin and towel) make up two of the four symbols in the BIC logo.

CONCLUSION

I return to my story from the Grand Canyon where I stood with people from around the world, eager to capture the fleeting beauty of the sunset. It was a pale shadow of the vision from Revelation 7: throngs from all nations and languages will stand and cry out in praise before the One who created all things: "Amen! Blessing and glory and wisdom and thanksgiving and honor and power and might be to our God forever and ever! Amen!" (Revelation 7:9–12).[16] May our worship as BIC churches recalibrate us into vibrant, Spirit-empowered Jesus followers. May we be faithful and intentional in our planning so that the transforming work of God flows through us and transforms the world around us, for the sake of God's Kingdom.

. . . .

RESPONSE ESSAY

Worshiping God

▶ *Ericka Henry, Allentown, Pennsylvania*

Holy District BIC is a young, multicultural faith community in Allentown, Pennsylvania. Planted in the spring of 2019, our community has grown roots in the most ethnically diverse and socioeconomically disadvantaged zip code of our city. While God has certainly provided a range of gifts, passions, and strengths within our planting team and worshiping community, we do not currently serve with any who are musically inclined, nor does our liturgy include a traditional sermon and song set combination. Yet we continue to see life transformation, new believers coming to faith, and steady (albeit slow) maturation among the Christ followers in our community. As a believer who grew up in church services blessed with beautifully-led songs and stirring sermons, I have been delighted to discover that heartfelt worship can also be experienced in a God-honoring and Spirit-directed way when neither of these forms of worship are present, or even pursued.

The essay for this core value reflects on a number of principles for worship which may shape the BIC church for the twenty-first century, sharing how these principles can enable diverse congregations in an ever-changing culture to be united and formed in our heartfelt worship of God. Two particular principles resonate most with the Holy District experience of worship: extending hospitality and encouraging active participation. Our focus on these two principles has enabled us to worship as a multilingual congregation at every stage of our growth process and has graced us with a number of powerful testimonies. As a worshiping community we are learning to lean in and corporately practice our BIC core values.

EXTENDING HOSPITALITY

Our beginnings as a pioneer church plant oriented us toward hospitality from the onset. Our early gatherings prioritized connecting with neighbors who were unchurched or de-churched, taking into consideration the cultural divide between those who are comfortable in church settings and those who are not. We created two distinct gathering opportunities—one community gathering designed solely to cultivate spaces of belonging and connection in our neighborhood, and one worship gathering designed solely for believers who desired to grow in their faith and their sentness to their neighborhood. This differentiation of space positioned our planting team (three people in our early stages) to overcome those cultural barriers in community gatherings and build meaningful relationships with our neighbors.

As those relationships grew, so did curiosity about our motives, interest in spiritual conversations, and individual desire to follow Jesus. One of our current board members, Carlos, was an atheist when he first attended one of our community gatherings. It only took eight months, the power of the Holy Spirit, and the beauty of Jesus to bring Carlos to confess faith in Jesus, pursue baptism, and join our worshiping gathering. Since the beginning, our planting team has understood our service at community gatherings as an act of worship—one way in which we bow before our Lord and offer our time and gifts in service to his kingdom.

ENCOURAGING ACTIVE PARTICIPATION

Carlos is one of many who found their way from our community gathering into our intergenerational worship gathering, which is characterized by active participation. If one were to join us on any given Sunday morning, you might wonder if church were really happening. We begin our liturgy at different times every week, though officially it starts at 11:00 a.m., depending on when our community members filter in. Once our people have arrived and greeted everyone with a kiss, we read a passage of scripture and a prayer aloud together, in Spanish first and then in English. This reading is followed by a time for personal prayer and reflection and then concluded with a conversation that we like to think of as confession. It is a time to tell the truth about ourselves, our relationship to God, others, and the text we read, and how the Spirit is speaking to us as we read communally. This conversation is always unpredictable, requiring translation and patience across the community, and often surfaces questions, fears, or tearful realizations. It is especially important to those in our community who can speak both English and Spanish but struggle to read in either language. The final elements of our worship liturgy include communion and a closing reflection on our place as missionaries in our everyday lives.

PRACTICING BIC VALUES

Spread throughout our community and worship gatherings are opportunities to live out our BIC values in natural and winsome ways. Our growing worshiping community is being continually sent out to bear witness to the good news of King Jesus. Embedded as we are in the neighborhood, we have countless opportunities to pursue peace amid conflict on the block. We gather around scripture to learn from our Teacher and seek to obey him as he sends us to serve one another and our neighborhood.

Since participating in our early community gatherings, a team of grandmothers in our community have taken the lead on serving compassionately in our neighborhood. They are throwing ice cream parties for neighborhood kids, hosting neighborhood meetings, and planning ways to love and serve the unhoused community in our city—all while caring for aging parents, grandkids, spouses, and neighbors in their day-to-day lives. I credit our emphasis on active participation in every aspect of worship for the sense of agency and urgency that these women display as an expression of their faith in Jesus.

CONCLUSION

When curiosity arose from those first community gatherings, one of the most common questions we received from our neighbors once they learned I was a pastor was this: "Well, when are you going to start doing church, then?" Time after time, I simply answered with a smile, "We already are." And while I believed this then, I believe it more now. I am grateful to God that he has provided the opportunity for our motley crew to experience heartfelt worship that is God-honoring, Spirit-directed, and life transforming in the unusual way that we do: extending hospitality, encouraging active participations, and living out our BIC values.

• • • • • • • • • • • • • • • • • •

RESPONSE ESSAY
Worshiping God
▶ *Sindah Ngulube, Bulawayo, Zimbabwe*

Whereas it is true that our environs shape us, whether consciously or not, we are to be transformed by worship, quieting disturbing noises through the power of worship in our own cultural context. In other words, we must be disciplined and say *no* to anything that is ungodly for us to experience transformation in worship (Titus 2:11).

CONNECTING TO THE GLOBAL BODY OF CHRIST

Twenty-first century communication platforms give us easy access to connecting with others around the world. Someone from Africa can communicate with those in North America in real time. This is a very good way of sharing the gospel throughout the world with few limitations, though Africa still lags in technological infrastructure. However, while it may mean being able to connect and worship with people in far countries, it may also more easily allow us to ignore the person sitting right next to us. Overall, global connectivity has brought spiritual growth and broader understanding of God's grace across race and ethnicity within the body of Christ.

The internet can help Christians in Africa access the Bible, communicate with each other, share their faith, and learn from other Christians around the world.[17] For example, the YouVersion Bible app has been installed more than 260 million times worldwide and offers many translations and languages, including several African languages, such as SiNdebele and ChiShona, languages used predominantly in Zimbabwe.[18]

Technology can also pose some threats and challenges to the African church, such as biblical illiteracy, lack of presence, consumerism, individualism, and syncretism.[19] For example, some Christians may rely on their phone or social media more than on the Word of God or the community of believers. The African church needs to be proactive in discerning internet use for the glory of God and the edification of the body of Christ. By teaching and modeling biblical literacy, presence, stewardship, and unity, the church can help direct its people. Also, as the church engages with the culture and the society around it in relevant and faithful ways, the use of technology must be seen as a tool and not an idol.

EXTENDING HOSPITALITY

In Africa, hospitality is an important part of our culture. One way BIC churches in Zimbabwe extend hospitality is by planning and organizing visitor days. A visitor's day at a local BIC church is an opportunity to welcome new attendees and those who may be attending but have not committed to Christ or membership. The goal is to make individuals aware of BIC principles. On visitor days, a message may focus on the mission of the church, based on the teaching of Matthew 28:19–20. Visitors are invited to introduce themselves or share their testimonies during the service or to join a small group or a fellowship lunch after the service.

BIC Zimbabwe extends hospitality during the Africa Sunday Service on Africa Day, May 25th. Many churches modify this celebration to be a time of extending hospitality to the entire community, welcoming unchurched people. Invitations are sent to people throughout the community, and everyone is encouraged to wear their African attire to the event. On that day, African dishes are prepared and shared, African

Christian songs are sung, and a short message about the love of God sending his Son into the world to rescue the lost people is preached targeting the unchurched visitors. At the end of the service people are invited for food and refreshments while having fellowship.

TELLING GOD'S STORY

Sometimes it is a challenge to spread the gospel. As we tell God's story in Africa, messages from the prosperity gospel often mislead the people. The prosperity gospel message is portrayed as a promise of God's blessing and favor for those who believe and obey him. Also known as the health and wealth gospel, the name it and claim it gospel, or the positive confession gospel, the overarching message says that God wants his children to prosper in every area of life, including finances, health, relationships, and career. It also teaches that faith is a force that can activate God's power and that positive words can create positive realities.[20]

Many people are drawn to the prosperity gospel message in Zimbabwe because of the harsh realities of poverty, suffering, unemployment, and health problems faced by the population. The prosperity gospel offers them a hope of escaping their situation and achieving their dreams. It also appeals to their cultural worldview, which values material wealth, success, and status as signs of God's favor and protection. Further, it resonates with their spiritual hunger, which seeks for signs, wonders, and miracles as evidence of God's presence and power.[21]

As BIC Zimbabwe, we refute the prosperity gospel by affirming that God loves and cares for all people, especially the poor and the marginalized, and that God calls his people to do the same. We also teach that suffering is not a sign of

God's curse or lack of faith, but a reality that can be transformed by God's power and presence.

As BIC churches, our strength is in the Christian education classes held every Sunday for all age groups, where scripture is studied together prior to the main service. Home Cell Groups are also opportunities to study the Bible together. Everyone is taught and encouraged to tell God's story.

In the Zimbabwean context, a perspective that captures the principles of worship aligned with BIC core values is what some scholars term the African Christian theology of Ubuntu. Ubuntu is a philosophy and a way of life that emphasizes the interconnectedness and interdependence of all human beings. It means *I am because we are* or *humanity towards others*. It is a theology of life, care, solidarity, economic justice, hope, and accompaniment.

Within this understanding, God is the source and the giver of life, and God's blessing is not measured by material possessions, but by the quality of relationships with God and with others. God's blessing is also not limited to individuals but extends to the whole community and all of creation (Genesis 12:2). Further, God's blessing is not earned by faith or works but is a gift of grace that is freely given to all (Ephesians 2:8–9). Lastly, God's blessing is not hoarded or consumed but is shared and multiplied. God's blessing is not used for selfish gain, but for the common good and the glory of God.[22]

· · · · · · · · · · · · · · · · · ·

CHAPTER 3

Discussion Questions

1. In what way(s) does our worship not honor God? How can we recalibrate our hearts to God in worship?

2. In what way(s) is our worship centered on the individual? How can we focus our worship on the community of faith?

3. How does your community of faith interact with one another during worship? Is everyone invited to participate and contribute within the gathering?

4. Is your worship grounded in Scripture? Do you use the Psalms in worship gatherings? How might we use the Old and New Testament readings in worship to reshape our imaginations?

5. How have you experienced the two BIC ordinances of baptism and the Lord's Supper? What significance do each have for you within the community of faith?

CHAPTER 4

Following Jesus

Danisa Ndlovu

*We value wholehearted obedience to Christ Jesus
through the empowering presence of the Holy Spirit.*

INTRODUCTION: JESUS CALLING

We live in a very complex world. So many voices call for our attention and allegiance. Confusion is normative and truth is relative. And yet, cutting through the noise is the voice of a God who speaks. Into the midst of the original formless chaos God speaks, and the Spirit of God hovering over the waters brings form and shape through a spoken word (Genesis 1:1). Throughout the Scripture story God continues to speak, through individual men and women, prophets, kings, and judges. Ultimately, the Word that gave form to creation took on flesh in the person of Jesus. In John chapter one, we read about the incarnation of Jesus Christ. That incarnation is well summarized in verse 14, "And the Word became flesh and lived among us, and we have seen his glory, the glory as of a father's only son, full of grace and truth." Christ Jesus became incarnate as the definitive revelation of the nature and character of God. The voice of Jesus of Nazareth cuts through the noise of the gods of every age as the fullest representation of the being and nature of God (Hebrews 1:4).

The same voice of Jesus that called out to the first disciples continues to call out to us. The message is simple, but the implications are all encompassing. To Simon Peter and his brother Andrew, Jesus said "Come, follow me!" (Matthew 4:19 NIV). Their response? "At once they left their nets and followed him" (Matthew 4:20 NIV).

And yet, they did not know what lay ahead. All they knew was who they were following. Being a disciple of Jesus does not mean following a plan but following a person. Plans are meant to be accomplished, a person is meant to be known and trusted. The plan is God's to accomplish, Jesus is who we are called to know. Particularly, we are called to know his voice. *Following Jesus* means recognizing the voice of Jesus and following where that voice leads.

FOLLOWING THE VOICE OF THE GOOD SHEPHERD

The BIC say, "We value wholehearted obedience to Christ," and this kind of obedience begins through the grace of learning the voice of the one whom we obey.[1] In the gospel of John, the disciple writes, he goes on ahead of them, and his sheep follow him because they know his voice (John 10:27). *Following Jesus* means learning to listen to the voice of Jesus, and we learn to listen to the voice of Jesus by observing how Jesus listened for the voice of his Father.

As Jesus was baptized, the gospel of Matthew says, "At that moment heaven was opened, and he saw the Spirit of God descending like a dove and lighting on him. And a voice from heaven said, 'This is my Son, whom I love; with him I am

well pleased'" (Matthew 3:16–17 NIV). As BIC, we believe we
receive the gift of the indwelling of the Holy Spirit upon our
baptism. This is the moment of surrender where we respond
to the heavenly knock and open the door to the filling of the
Holy Spirit. As John records Jesus saying, "You know him
[Holy Spirit], for he lives with you and will be in you" (John
14:17 NIV). It is through the Holy Spirit that the Father and
Son dwell within us. Just a few verses later Jesus says, "Anyone
who loves me will obey my teaching. My Father will love them,
and *we* will come to them and make our home with them"
(John 14:23 NIV, emphasis added). God's home is made in us
through the Holy Spirit, who guides us in the ways of Jesus.

We may not often think of this, but Jesus lived a life led by
the Holy Spirit. The beauty of Jesus' life was how he listened
for the leading of the Holy Spirit, and how he depended on
the power of the Holy Spirit. How do you think it was that he
did what he saw the Father doing, or said what he heard the
Father saying? It was because Jesus received the Holy Spirit
and chose, each moment, to "keep in step with the Spirit"
(Galatians 5:25 NIV). Sometimes we emphasize the divinity
of Jesus to the diminishment of his humanity. When we do
this, we diminish his identification with us, and the beautiful
identification we can have with him. As we follow Jesus, we
learn to listen as Jesus listened.

Listening for the voice of Jesus will lead us to remote places,
distanced from the hustle and bustle of life. Jesus needed time
alone, time away from the crowds and the demands others put
on him to listen for the direction of his Father. But do not mis-
take listening for a place or location absent of noise. Yes, those
things are helpful, but they are only a means to a greater end.
The objective of finding places of quiet is not only to silence
the outer world, but the inner world as well. Hearing the voice

of the Good Shepherd comes from a quiet heart. The psalmist did not just write about quiet places (Psalm 23), but also the quieting of himself (Psalm 131). *Following Jesus* means quieting ourselves for the sake of communion with God.

Learning to listen

Oftentimes Christians become frustrated with their inability to hear God. Part of that frustration comes as a result of struggling to find a place of both outer and inner quiet. Perhaps there is no "remote place" to find. Perhaps the silence of remote places causes the mind to race, and the quiet leads to anxiousness, and the feeling of anxiousness feels like failure of the time spent seeking God in silence. All of this results in feelings of frustration or even failure, and so the pursuit of quiet places to listen for Jesus is abandoned altogether.

Remember, when the disciples set out to follow Jesus, they had no idea where they were going. All they knew was *who* they were following. Where they were going and what they would be doing was yet to be revealed, and it would never be revealed all at once. Learning to listen to the voice of Jesus is not all that different.

Many of us give up too soon. We have an impression that the voice of God or the direction of God is going to thunder from the clouds. God's message will be written in the sky! Perhaps, but rarely. Read through the scriptures and see that our forebears in the faith struggled and wrestled to hear and listen to God, too. Struggling and wrestling was part of learning, part of what it meant to follow. To listen to another person is to learn who they are, to know them more deeply. One conversation never reveals everything about a person. Even after decades of conversations, spouses can learn something new as they listen to each other.

Listening for the voice of Jesus is not primarily about an answer. Sometimes God graces us with answers when we ask a question, but we must move past simply listening for answers if we are to move more deeply into *Following Jesus*. In the gospels Jesus rarely answers a question. What does he do? He asks another question. Yes, this is the rabbinical method of teaching during that time, but it is also formative. Jesus did not just want people to have the right answers, he wanted them to become the right kind of people. Becoming the right kind of people takes a long time. It takes a lifetime.

Listening for the voice of Jesus is for the sake of knowing Jesus. And Jesus wants to be known!

Ways we hear God
What does the voice of God sound like? What should we listen for? How will we know it's God? These are all big questions, but we are not left without ways of thinking about them. The following are a few simple suggestions to guide our thinking of what it means to listen to God.

It will sound like Jesus. The BIC are centered on the person of Jesus. We believe, as the New Testament attests, that Jesus is the fullest revelation and representation of God (John 1; Colossians 1:15–20; Hebrews 1:1–3). Therefore, whatever we think we hear Jesus saying we must also see Jesus doing. We learn what Jesus would (or would not) do by immersing ourselves in the gospels, learning the voice and character of Jesus through the accounts of Jesus. Anything at odds with the Jesus revealed in the gospels must be questioned. A simple question we can ask ourselves is this: Would Jesus do or say what I think I am hearing from God?

Jesus as the lens for reading Scripture. As BIC, we value *Believing the Bible* and read it as one of the primary means of God's communication. However, we do not read the Bible flatly. We do not deem a verse taken from the Old Testament to carry equal weight as a word from Jesus. This is because we read the Bible as a progressive revelation culminating in the ultimate revelation of Jesus Christ as the Son of God. Jesus is the end to which we read the Scriptures. As we listen for the voice of God in the Scripture, we pay attention to the voice of Christ.

The Anabaptism at 500 project invited Anabaptist churches throughout the world to contribute to the Anabaptist Community Bible. Churches who formed small groups and chose to participate were given three scriptures and five questions. One of the questions: "What would Jesus have to say about this passage?"[2] What a question! This question guides our reading of Scripture as we listen to how God speaks through Scripture.

Community. Lastly, as BIC, we believe we hear God through the community of faith. There are moments in the scripture where individuals have gone to the mountaintop and received words from God, but they are by far the exception to the rule (and we should be cautious of leaders or individuals for whom this is their norm). Instead, it was through the oral tradition, sitting around synagogues and living rooms, where people read and discerned the scriptures together.

We call this a community hermeneutic. Imagine the beauty and power of sitting in a circle of brothers and sisters, reading the scriptures together, and hearing how we hear Jesus through the scripture. Each person represents a different perspective based on gender, race, economics, family history, personality, influences, and so on. And every person, as followers of Jesus, is filled with the Spirit! We encounter the Holy Spirit as we encounter each other. We listen to the voice of the Holy Spirit as we listen to each other. And as we listen together, we are centered, once again, on Jesus.

FOLLOWING IN OBEDIENCE

Following Jesus means obeying what we hear. The BIC have been shaped by Anabaptism. Anabaptism began around the time of Martin Luther's Reformation. The Anabaptist movement would be referred to as the Radical Reformation, taking Luther's reformations even a step farther. Central to the Anabaptist understanding of following Jesus was obedience, first into the waters of baptism, and then through the way one lived. For Anabaptists, salvation was not just what Jesus did for you, but how you lived obediently in response to Jesus. Conversion was not only a moment, but a life-long transformation into Christlikeness. Like the radical change of Andrew and Peter, Anabaptists believed there were "boats to be left behind." Jesus was to be obediently followed.

And Jesus was one who obediently followed! We learn how to follow in obedience by paying attention to how Jesus followed in obedience. Christ's devotion to his Father according to the scripture is obvious and unquestionable. He spoke only what his Father commanded him to say (John 12:49). He only did what he saw his Father doing (John 5:19). He purposed and subjected his will to that of his Father who sent him (John 5:30; John 6:38–40). This is devotion par excellence! No part of Jesus was left to operate independent of God. His love and loyalty to his Father consumed his total being, causing Jesus to be an example of what it means to live a life of obedience to God—an example for his followers.

Statistics in Zimbabwe suggest that 80 to 90 percent of our population claim to be Christian.[3] But when you see the levels of corruption, forms of violence, disregard for human life and other ills affecting our nation, they all demonstrate that in today's world the term *Christian* is not synonymous to being a true follower of Jesus Christ, since people who are committing those evil acts are among that 80 to 90 percent bracket. Being a follower of Christ requires a radical change of character and therefore a behavior which stands in direct contrast with the common attitudes and behaviors of the majority.

I once had a conversation with one of my former students who is serving in ministry. He told me his siblings are doing well in life. Some are lawyers, some hold high positions in government departments, and some are in other trades. They drive expensive cars. "I am the only one who appears to be struggling in life with taking care of myself and family," he said. "Do I regret that I am in ministry? Not at all. I have always known from the beginning that ministry is self-sacrifice. That is my cost of following Jesus," he concluded.

For this student, obedience to Christ was not a burden but a service of thanksgiving to God. They had an appreciation that while they were yet sinners, Christ died for them (Romans 5:8). They came to know that God's favor was given to us independent of what we do but simply because God in Christ loved us—while we were yet sinners! In Ephesians, Paul emphatically says, "And this is not your own doing; it is the gift of God—not the result of works, so that no one may boast. For we are what he has made us, created in Christ Jesus for good works, which God prepared beforehand so that we may walk in them," (Ephesians 2:8–10 NRSVue).

It is good to be reminded that obedience comes as a response to God's gift of salvation. At times, the church has exchanged joyful obedience for demanding duty. When this happened, obedience to Christ became obedience to norms set forth by the church. Unfortunately for many Christians these experiences left them confused, not knowing how to differentiate between following a person or an institution and following Christ. To follow and to blindly obey the leader of their church was understood as following Christ. They knew the voice of their leader, but they hardly know the voice of Jesus our Lord.

This is a humbling reminder and encouragement to the leaders of our church to be women and men who help the sheep under our care to follow the voice of the Good Shepherd, because *Following Jesus* means learning what his voice sounds like. It is also a good reminder to the laypeople of the church: anyone who speaks on behalf of God must point to Jesus, through their words, their actions, and their life.

FOLLOWING JESUS AS A PART OF THE CHURCH

Following Jesus is never done alone. It is done alongside. To follow Jesus is to be human; to accept and attach with one another. Together as brothers and sisters we respond to Jesus' invitation, "Follow me" (Matthew 4:19).

One of the ways Jesus helps us experience and celebrate this brotherhood and sisterhood is by gathering around the table in response to the invitation and work of Jesus in communion. It is there where bonding is experienced, and sin is exposed. We examine ourselves through the Spirit of God not so that we can be deemed worthy based on our works, but to receive mercy based upon God's desire to share it. It is at the communion table where we celebrate the human Jesus who shed his blood for the remission of our sins.

At the communion table the church, as it follows Jesus, makes a declaration that it is not ashamed of brokenness. It is in brokenness that we become useful to one another. Painful as that may be, it is in brokenness that we find our strength through the power of the Holy Spirit. It is in our brokenness that Jesus meets us. In brokenness we are most vulnerable and able to share who we are and what we desire to become as we follow Christ Jesus.

It is in our experience of brokenness that we find equality. This experience of brokenness around the communion table illustrates what Paul describes, saying, "For in Christ Jesus you are all children of God through faith. As many of you as were baptized into Christ have clothed yourselves with Christ. There is no longer Jew or Greek, there is no longer slave or free, there is no longer male and female; for all of you are one in Christ Jesus," (Galatians 3:26–28). In simple terms Paul is saying that as Christians we are all equal in the eyes of God.

Those who join around this table, locally and globally, are the ones God will bring to minister to us. They are ones through whom the Spirit will speak. These are people who will accompany and encourage us; teach and admonish us. They will come with their various gifts to help grow into the like-ness of Christ. In our culture we have a saying that it takes a village to raise a child.[4] This is also true in the Christian family. It takes a community of believers to raise a young believer to Christian maturity, and the young believers to keep the mature in humility. Paul recognized this when he said, "We have gifts that differ according to the grace given to us: prophecy, in pro-portion to faith; ministry, in ministering; the teacher, in teach-ing; the encourager, in encouragement; the giver, in sincerity; the leader, in diligence; the compassionate, in cheerfulness" (Romans 12:6–8 NRSVue).

Ministry to one another, through the Spirit, leads one another to freedom. Christ's followers are those who have been freed from legalism. Can you envision this—communi-ties of faith guiding one another into greater freedom?! As

Paul writes, "Now the Lord is the Spirit, and where the Spirit of the Lord is, there is freedom" (2 Corinthians 3:17). Their lives are no longer shaped by the patterns of this world. Meeting together regularly, their hearts and minds continue to be transformed as they discern and articulate what God desires of us and the world (Romans 12:2). John calls it being "born again" (John 3:3 NIV). Paul speaks of it as putting "away your former way of life, your old self, corrupt and deluded by its lusts, and to be renewed in the spirit of your minds, and to clothe yourselves with the new self, created according to the likeness of God in true righteousness and holiness" (Ephesians 4:22–24). Followers of Christ are no longer shaped by the patterns of this world in the manner they live and conduct themselves; rather they are shaped to be like God in that they exhibit the things that Jesus taught and did.

FOLLOWING JESUS INTO THE WORLD
Faithful men and women of the Bible served and trusted God in very difficult political, economic, social and religious environments. Jesus makes the invitation to follow him in a context similar to ours. The government was ruthless and oppressive. The religious leaders made a show of themselves and were condemned as hypocrites. The have and have-nots were there. The clean, unclean, mentally challenged, and the demonic were part of society. Following Jesus did not mean fleeing the world, but engaging the world for Christ's sake, being in but not of the world (John 17:13–19).

Following God's kingdom in the midst of the world
The Anabaptist tradition of the BIC strongly believes there are two kingdoms that influence our existence in the world. There is the kingdom of this world that has influence over those who

are born of the flesh, have a carnal mind, and in general pursue things that do not please God. Then there is the kingdom of God/Christ comprised of those who are regenerated and live by the Spirit of God. Followers of Christ belong to this peaceful kingdom and will not use earthly weapons to fight their wars but rather use spiritual weapons (Ephesians 6:10–18) to obtain eternal rewards.

Following Jesus is not aligning to any political system but standing and devoting oneself to righteousness. It is courageously speaking truth to power whenever necessary without apology. Sometimes this can easily cause division and misunderstandings even within close family members (Luke 14:26–27), dissensions (Titus 3:9–11), abandonment (Psalm 27:10), and feelings of rejection (John 15:18; Luke 10:16), as well as loss of income and other life sustaining resources (Luke 18:28). Scripture is also very clear that those who stand for truth are likely to be persecuted. But when that happens, we "do not worry about how you are to speak or what you are to say; for what you are to say will be given to you at that time; for it is not you who speak, but the Spirit of your Father speaking through you" (Matthew 10:19–20).

What is of concern today is how our church leaders align themselves to political systems of the time. In the process, they are corrupted and become agents of the evil rulers of our time. Tendai Ruben Mpofana, in his article "Zimbabwe Churches Turn Evil, Please Jesus Come Back," expressed his indignation about how the church in Zimbabwe enjoys sharing a blanket with evil politicians and a corrupt political system in the country. He is concerned when:

Various Christian leaders transform their church gatherings into political rallies—where brutal oppressive thieving politicians are permitted to freely use pulpits as campaign platforms. . . . If Christians are now willing agents of the devil, as they promote corrupt ruthless politicians, what image of Jesus Christ are they portraying to the world? Truly God-fearing leaders will never persecute, abuse and brutalize the same people our Heavenly Father has appointed them to lead. . . . Where are the genuine followers and believers of Christ—when evil men are taking over the Body of Christ—bringing all manner of criminals and gangster to parade themselves as "appointed by God," and as such worthy of support.[5]

This is not unique to Zimbabwe.

One of the most difficult and challenging areas in following Christ is in recognizing the power of the gospel in bringing down the racial, tribal, class, and religious walls. Emmanuel Katongole states a piercing truth, "Christian expression throughout the world has too easily allowed the blood of tribalism to flow deeper than the waters of baptism."[6] Followers of Christ who enjoy the benefits of racial and tribal divisions, etc., must pause and seriously think about their faith and commitment to Christ.

Paul, in the book of Ephesians, did not mince his words when he said,

For he is our peace; in his flesh he has made both groups [Jew and Gentile] into one and has broken down the dividing wall, that is, the hostility between us. . . so that he might create in himself one new humanity in place of the two, thus making peace, and might reconcile both groups to God in one body through the cross, thus putting to death that hostility through it. So he. . . proclaimed peace to you who were far off and peace to those who were near; for through him both of us have access in one Spirit to the Father. (Ephesians 2:14–18)

We cannot be free until we make right the injustices we have committed toward other people. The presence of the church, by her very nature, her relationship to Christ in this corrupt world, prick the consciences of those who are using their authority to suppress and exploit others. Our witness challenges those who oppress to accept and confess their sin humbly and voluntarily. A true church of Jesus Christ strongly stands against any forms of oppression, and systems that promote inequality especially at the expense of the poor and marginalized. It must always remain a voice of the voiceless. Let us never forget the words of Christ, "Truly I tell you, just as you did it to one of the least of these who are members of my family, you did it to me" (Matthew 25:40).

CONCLUSION

Christ Jesus became incarnate in order to know and experience what it means to live faithful to God in a sinful and hostile world. Jesus saved us by remaining faithful to God, serving, and saving a creation at enmity with God. The followers of Christ must learn from his example: that is, if they are to be of any service to the world they need to be seen as "incarnate" in and by the people among whom they live. Only then can the church be viewed as identifying with those in the margins of our societies, the poor, the sick, the homeless, the prisoners, the needy and voiceless. According to Matthew 25: 31–46, *Following Jesus* is in serving "the least of these." The incarnated church is one that is willing to sacrifice all it has for the well-being of God's people both physically and spiritually. For the most part this remains a dream for today's church.

Just as Christ incarnate was rejected by his own people, the followers of Christ must be prepared to suffer rejection and humiliation for doing good, but remain steadfast in loving the world as much as God loved it. The church that fails to be incarnate among its people loses its saltiness and its light soon flickers off and becomes part of the dark world.

. . . .

RESPONSE ESSAY

Following Jesus

▶ *Perry Engle, Upland, California*

Following Jesus is at the very heart of our BIC core values—the sum of our identity, and the goal of our calling.

Dietrich Bonhoeffer observed that "Follow me" was the first and last word Jesus spoke to Peter (Matthew 4:19; John 21:22). I would contend that it remains his first and last word to *every believer.* In my mind, these two words—"Follow me"—remain the two most important words in all of Scripture.

HEARING JESUS' CALLING

Jesus' call to "follow me" is the essence of what it means to be a Christian. I first heard this call at the age of ten, and then in a more pronounced way, at summer camp at the age of fifteen. My call to follow Christ was not so much a call *towards* something; it was a call *away* from my former life—a life of arrogance, and self-reliance, and pleasure—and a call to the very person of Christ. For me, to hear Jesus calling was literally a call to die to myself. To take up my cross and follow him.

In college, I sensed a call to follow Jesus into ministry. I had no idea what that meant, except that the church would somehow become the vehicle through which my pursuit of Jesus would take place. It remains a sad assumption that *Following Jesus* is done primarily through vocational ministry. To me, nothing could be farther from the truth. "Whatever you do," writes Paul, "whether in word or deed, do it all in the name of the Lord Jesus, giving thanks to God the Father through him" (Colossians 3:17 NIV). Following Jesus means hearing and pursuing whatever call he has placed on our individual lives.

THE VOICE OF THE GOOD SHEPHERD

What beautiful, intimate language John uses in the tenth chapter of his gospel: "The shepherd. . . calls his own sheep by name and leads them out. When he has brought out all his own, he goes on ahead of them, and his sheep follow him because they know his voice" (John 10:2–4 NIV).

I discovered early on in ministry that Jesus, the Good Shepherd, is the lens through which I read Scripture and hear his voice. I recently suggested to a Hebraic-centric Christian brother, in a somewhat heated online discussion, that as Christians we *always* look at the Old Testament through the lens of Christ, and not vice versa. The reason for this is because Jesus is the fullest representation of God that we have—the incarnate Word (John 1:14), the image of the invisible God, the firstborn over all creation (Colossians 1:15), and the One who has made God known (John 1:18). "In the past," writes the author of Hebrews, "God spoke to our ancestors through the prophets at many times and in various ways, but in these last days he has spoken to us by his Son," who is "the exact representation of his being" (Hebrews 1:1–3 NIV).

Learning to hear the Good Shepherd's voice means that I allow him to lead me through the corridors of both the Old and New Testaments and understand that every page of Scripture speaks of Jesus (Luke 24:27) and teaches how I am to follow him.

FOLLOWING IN OBEDIENCE, AS A PART OF THE CHURCH

Rugged individualism, as much as it is a part of the American ethos, is not the way to follow Jesus. *Following Jesus* is always done as a part of the community of believers. It is how we are kept accountable, obtain wisdom, interpret the Bible, and remain humble. Community is our hermeneutic, as well as our means of following Jesus.

Following Jesus in obedience infers that it is not enough to just believe the right doctrine, but also that I do what the Bible says in a way Jesus would do it. To follow Jesus in obedience means that I am not only a hearer of the word, but a doer of the word as well (James 1:22–25).

FOLLOWING JESUS INTO THE WORLD

Sincere, thoughtful believers have asked Marta and me (as gently as possible) how we can live in a place like California. The inference, of course, is that it must be horrible, and terribly compromising, to live and minister in a place as liberal and godless and secular as the Golden State. We always have a relatively straightforward answer to people who wonder about the seriousness of our faith because of where we live: We have followed Jesus, and Jesus has led us here—me as a lead pastor of a 120-year-old congregation, and Marta as a public school teacher.

As we follow Jesus, he has called us to engage with this broken world, not escape it. Jesus prayed quite purposefully for his disciples, the first Jesus followers: "My prayer is not that you take them out of the world but that you protect them from the evil one. . . . As you sent me into the world, I have sent them into the world" (John 17:15, 18 NIV).

Following Jesus means that we are incarnationally encamped in a broken and needy world. It means we are called to minister to the least of these (Matthew 25:31–46), stand for peace and justice, and boldly proclaim the Word of God without compromise.

Jesus is at the very heart of our BIC core values. That's a good thing, but it's not nearly enough.

Following Jesus should be at the very heart of every person who calls themselves a Christian. Following Jesus should be the sum of our individual identities—not conjoined with any political, national, cultural, ethnic, or sexual identity.

Being a follower of Jesus should never be just a *part* of who I am.

It will always be, first and foremost, *who I am.*

"Follow me" will always be Christ's first and last word to anyone who has ears to hear.

· · · · · · · · · · · · · · · · · ·
RESPONSE ESSAY
Following Jesus
▶ *Sibonokuhle Ncube, Goshen, Indiana*

> **Somlandel' uJesu/We Will Follow Jesus**
> Somlandela, somlandel' uJesu.
> Somlandela yonke indawo.
> Somlandela, somlandel' uJesu.
> Lapho eyakhona somlandela.
>
> We will follow, we will follow Jesus.
> We will follow, ev'rywhere he goes.
> We will follow, we will follow Jesus.
> Ev'rywhere he goes we will follow.

INTRODUCTION

"Somlandel' uJesu/We Will Follow Jesus"[7] looped through my thoughts with a beautiful resonance and cadence when I heard about the opportunity to reflect on the Brethren in Christ church value of *Following Jesus* from a global community perspective. "Somlandel' uJesu" was sung frequently at the Mennonite World Conference of 2003, which was hosted by the BIC church in my home city of Bulawayo, Zimbabwe.[8]

"Somlandel' uJesu" brought together the individual and communal joy of the multinational and multicultural congregation of Anabaptists who traveled from all over the world during a protracted socioeconomic crisis in Zimbabwe. Whilst the assembly sang and danced to this song and others, one could perceive that this was not a charade but a singular, passionate heartbeat for Christ-oriented living and mission. "Somlandel' uJesu" consolidated the identity, collective aspiration, and promise of the church as the incarnate body of Christ. The song gave the assembly an opportunity to recommit and identify with the bold Jesus-oriented movement the BIC church has historically embedded.

INVOKING IMAGINATION

Read closely, the lyrics of the song are both exciting and pithy, as they are shorthand for rhetoric and responses to important questions that the essay articulates: Which Jesus are we following within an age of apostasy? How do we come to know Jesus? What are some of the spiritual disciplines that are marks of faithful followers? The lyrics are eclectic as they invoke a prophetic imagination.

Following Jesus universally transforms disciples from self-serving orientations to countercultural life-giving witness to the gospel of the love that births new believers to freedom in Christ. This love and freedom in Christ are a central message in the teaching and multiplication of disciples, who in loving response live separate from sin and in right relationship with God, neighbors, and creation. The pithiness of the song about following Jesus critiques and captures both the cost and complexities of faithfully following Jesus Christ. Hebrews 12:2 and the Christ Hymn in Philippians 2:5–11 are both clear that Jesus is a sterling example of costly obedience.

RESOLUTENESS

The biblical narrative, alongside examples modeled by Christian leaders, fans resoluteness in discipleship. Ronald J. Sider's iconic speech to the Mennonite World Conference Assembly in Strasbourg (1984), declared that Jesus followers as peacemakers needed to be careful of isolationist pacifism that is aloof and passive to violence and injustice.[9] Beyond the imperative to multiply disciples out of sorrow for lost souls and the joy of seeing people come to the light of Christ, Sider correctly believed in a gospel of care and resoluteness. The BIC continue to recognize Sider's critique about service to vulnerable and underserved others as they value *Following Jesus*.

The lyrics of "Somlandel' uJesu" and the embodied action of living as Jesus followers can be witnessed in several vignettes. Elisha, the younger prophet, steadfastly and tenaciously follows the older prophet Elijah (1 Kings 19:19–21), serving and co-ministering with Elijah before Elijah is supernaturally transported to heaven. The passionate determination of "Somlandel' uJesu," at Advent, can be energized by a Marian connection to Mary's radical *yes* to birthing Immanuel, the God-Man.[10] The Magnificat that Mary sings in response to the annunciation energizes our own responses as disciples today. We can be inspired to think about how our faith as followers of Jesus can bear the responsible social and spiritual characteristics of nonviolence, justice to the "least of these"[11] and concern for those who still need to hear the gospel.

Jesus' followers are invited to subversive liturgical responses that articulate costly surrender to Jesus' call and sending of itinerant disciples to all nations (Matthew 28:19–20). Those who sing, "Lapha eyakhona somlandela (Wherever he goes we will follow)" and other verses stating "Asiyikwesaba (We will not be afraid)" should also know who Jesus Christ is and what is required of them as committed followers on the move. Followers of Jesus Christ must not only have capacity to discern his voice but also actively yield to doing Jesus' bidding. This is not easy.

Resoluteness to do Jesus' bidding to the least of these can stimulate formation of new structures and dramatic institutional shifts. The BIC Compassionate and Development

Services (CDS) was established to extend tables of fellowship to churches and communities mainly in the western region of Zimbabwe. Humanitarian relief, disaster recovery assistance, and long-term community resilience strengthening work continues to date. This has assisted the church to witness to the love of God, shared in very few words yet powerfully co-creating with underserved intergenerational rural and urban communities. Ministry is through sustainable livelihood interventions in agriculture, community asset building and maintenance, peacebuilding, and creation care within the context of climate change. A highlight in the life of CDS was a Help Bank for assisting victims of Cyclone Idai that had made fatal landfall in the Eastern Highlands of Zimbabwe in 2019. CDS mobilized BIC congregations and their contiguous communities to contribute food and non-food items (FNFI) to assuage the desperate situation. A chasm of historic intertribal animosities was challenged by this deep gesture of solidarity and provisioning love.

CONCLUSION

As the essay explains, Jesus followers embody a resurrected co-identification with Jesus and his costly power-hermeneutics. Jesus-power is not polemic nor imperial. Jesus-power is redemptive, restorative, and communal—generously affirming hospitality and adoptive belonging of others to God's family, which includes the least of these and all who believe (Matthew 25:45). The goal of *Following Jesus* is to lovingly extend the kingdom reign of God as obediential worship. A yielded lifestyle, which imitatively draws from an ethical monotheism inspired by the person of Jesus as the center of accountability, is shaped and guided by the Holy Spirit and the Scriptures. This helps the church to navigate the broken and ever-changing contexts of the world toward God's apocalyptic and eschatological ends.

With yearning for God's already-but-not-yet kingdom to fully come,[12] following Jesus embodies the New Covenant. There is hope and help for this! From the perspective of Jesus' teaching and virtuous instruction in the Scriptures, all who profess to be followers are empowered to relinquish all lesser loyalties in exclusive favor of Jesus Christ by the power of the Holy Spirit.

. . . .

CHAPTER 4

Discussion Questions

1. Why is it important to keep in tension the divinity of Jesus with his humanity? What happens when one is emphasized over the other?

2. Which one of the three "ways we hear God" are most familiar to you or practiced in your community? Is there one you, or your community, might grow into more? How might you go about doing that?

3. In a world that is so heavily polarized due to various factors such as the geopolitical landscape, world economics, and religious differences, etc., how do we as followers of Christ, in practical terms, love God wholeheartedly and our neighbor as ourselves?

4. In the midst of highly militarized societies where everyone is pushed to be patriotic, how do we live in a way that demonstrates we belong to another kingdom other than this world?

5. What implications are there for the life of a believer to have Christ as our model and to walk in his footsteps?

Belonging to the Community of Faith

Rob Douglass and Naomi Smith

We value integrity in relationships and mutual accountability in an atmosphere of love, grace, and acceptance.

INTRODUCTION

In his song "Church (Take Me Back)," Michael Cochren describes *Belonging to the Community of Faith* as "more than an obligation/it's our foundation/the family of God." The chorus of the song declares:

> Take me back
> To the place that feels like home
> To the people I can depend on
> To the faith that's in my bones. . .
> Oh, I want to go to church.[1]

As beautiful as those words are, many of us could testify that the sentiments of this songwriter are becoming less common, even in Christian circles. The research indicates that 15 percent of American adults living today, around forty million people, have stopped going to church in the last thirty years.[2] Some have slipped away from regular church attendance because of a geographic move or the pull of competing activities. Others have intentionally left because of relational damage or lingering disappointments. Within this new reality, the BIC continue to affirm the importance of building and belonging to healthy congregations, declaring that "we value integrity in relationships and mutual accountability in an atmosphere of love, grace, and acceptance."[3]

THE CHURCH'S IDENTITY CRISIS

There are many reasons for decreasing attendance in local congregations today, and the problem is by no means unique to the BIC.[4] At the heart, it seems as though we are experiencing an identity crisis of sorts. How else can we make sense of the current attitude of so many Western Christians who understand participation in the community of faith as optional to the Christian life at best and potentially detrimental to the Christian life at worst?

This identity crisis is far more dangerous than it may first appear. John Stackhouse has poignantly observed,

> When we, the church, are confused about who we are and whose we are, we can become anything and anyone's. We can become a goose-stepping, Hitler saluting abomination, as we were in the middle of the last century in Germany. We can become a self-righteous, self-centered, and racist boot on the neck of our prostrate neighbors, as we were in South Africa until the end of apartheid. We can become a machete-wielding, genocidal horror, as we were in Rwanda, just recently. We can become a corpulent, self-important irrelevance, as we are in so much of America today. And we

can become a sad, shrunken ghost, pining for past glory and influence, as we are in Canada, Britain, and most of Europe.[5]

In light of what is at stake, it is crucial that we address this confusion and clarify who we are and whose we are. Only then might we better understand our present condition and discover a remedy.

A thin view of salvation

With regularity, we BIC mention our various historic streams of influence—Anabaptism, Pietism, Wesleyanism, and Evangelicalism—when we describe ourselves. While each of these movements has left its imprint on our current self-understanding, circumstances today suggest that we have either forgotten or neglected some of the key features of early Anabaptism. Our understanding of salvation and its relationship to the church is a prime example.

The early Anabaptists, like others in the Reformation, affirmed the doctrine of justification by faith through grace—no one can earn God's favor. The Reformation's emphasis on justification merged with another cultural force of the day, which was the growing emphasis on the individual. The result was two significant outcomes that would have made the early Anabaptists uncomfortable.

First, various theological concepts, including deliverance, reconciliation, restoration, healing, obedience, and even sanctification received less and less attention. Second, a new theological emphasis garnered more and more attention, particularly within the Western church—*personal salvation*. With these two developments, the experience of salvation was inseparably associated with justification, and essentially separated salvation from the community of faith.

The current situation of the BIC is more understandable when we realize that all the BIC streams of influence can be understood within their historical context as having an emphasis on the importance of individual salvation at their core. Pietism had its emphasis on the individual living a holy life. Those who follow Wesley emphasize the experience of each person having one's "heart strangely warmed," and evangelicals' focus has been on individuals being "born again." This means that as each new stream began to influence the BIC, a particular understanding of personal salvation was being reinforced.

In our present efforts to understand why people perceive little need for church today, it seems that at least part of the decline is due to the message that we have been preaching. For decades or perhaps longer, we have taught that what ultimately matters is that individuals experience salvation and that the only thing they need to do to be saved is "just believe." Yet we scratch our heads at the fact that so many people feel no need for the church, especially among those who are "saved." But they are doing exactly what we taught them was necessary—they are "just believing." If this assessment is correct, it seems that we are victims of our own success.

Rediscovering discipleship

Interestingly, these two points, 1) salvation being understood primarily if not exclusively as justification, and 2) the individual as having central importance, are precisely two of the issues where the early Anabaptists departed from their Protestant counterparts. While agreeing with the Reformers on the importance of justification, the early Anabaptists did not understand the *initial* experience of being made right with God to be the goal or totality of salvation. Rather, it was only salvation's beginning. For them, justification enables the more central goal of becoming disciples. In the words of Harold Bender, at the heart of the Anabaptist vision was "a new conception of the essence of Christianity as discipleship."[6]

Discipleship within early Anabaptism was not exactly the same as it is currently conceived. Today we tend to equate discipleship with personal spiritual formation. While there is certainly overlap between the two, they are distinct. For the early Anabaptists, being a disciple was not simply about each of us being the best Christian that we can personally be. Discipleship for our spiritual ancestors was a deliberate following of Jesus within the context of a covenant community in order to be more Christlike and to reflect him more clearly to the world. The role the community played in discipleship for early Anabaptists cannot be overstated. In the words of Mennonite historian Walter Klassen, "Anabaptists were convinced that the Christian was not capable of being a disciple by himself; rather that he needed the help and understanding of others to walk the steep and narrow way of life."[7]

This is not to suggest that either the individual dimension of salvation or the focus on justification is entirely wrong, since the cross clearly proclaims God's enormous investment in our personal salvation. Instead, it seems we have suffered from misplaced emphases. These emphases have introduced confusion about how the topics of salvation and the church relate to one another and have led us away from the course set by the early Anabaptists.

Rethinking the nature and mission of the church

In what follows, we will consider two models for understanding how salvation and the church relate to one another, derived from the work of Singaporean theologian Simon Chan. As we proceed, it may be helpful to note that the distinguishing characteristic between them is the "ultimate purpose" (also understood as goal, end, or *telos*) of each and the "means" to that end. This will become clearer momentarily.

Traditional or functional view of the church. The traditional view, commonly held by evangelical Christians in general and the Western BIC in particular, asserts that God's ultimate purpose in the world involves saving individuals. In this view, often called the Functional or Instrumental View, the church serves as God's primary tool to accomplish the goal of personal salvation:

God's Ultimate Purpose → Saving People

His Means to that End → Church

Two problems arise with this view. First, rather than connecting our understanding of salvation to the church, it separates them, often neglecting the church in the process. This neglect occurs in part because the church is really an arbitrary instrument that God has chosen to use. There is nothing inherently special about the church. God could have somehow chosen to use clouds or the chirping of birds to communicate his offer of salvation if he willed, but he chose to create the church for this purpose. In this view, the church does its part as those who belong to it provide faithful, Spirit-empowered witness to God's good news in Christ though word and deed.

Second, in order for this model to be correct, it must be able to answer an important question: Once you have received salvation (which is God's ultimate goal), why do you need the church? Certainly, one answer is something along the lines of obedience. Hebrews 10:25 teaches that we should not stop meeting together. Therefore, once you are saved, you should be a part of the church because it is what God expects. While

I (Rob) personally find this a sufficient reason for belonging to the community of faith, it is not terribly inspiring.

Another common response is that Christians ought to be a part of the church because the Christian life is too difficult to accomplish by oneself.[8] While it is true that the Christian life is extremely hard to live well alone, the reality seems to be even more stark. As was noted previously, the early Anabaptists did not think that it was too hard to live the Christian life well by oneself but that it was impossible to live the Christian life as Christ intended by oneself.

Ontological view of the church. This Functional View of the church has been questioned recently by Simon Chan.[9] In his book *Liturgical Theology,* Chan does not offer a new alternative to the Functional View. Rather, he calls for a return to what he believes to be a more basic, biblical, and historic understanding of the church and how the church relates to salvation. Chan's proposal seems to have something to offer the BIC today.

Chan calls his model an Ontological View of the church. Ontology is a philosophical term for discussing something's nature or essence. The difference between the two perspectives is a matter of focus. The Functional View focuses on what the church *does,* and the Ontological View is interested in who/ what the church *is.* The result of this move is that the end and the means have switched places.

Where the Functional View understood God's ultimate purpose as saving people *through the church,* the Ontological View sees God's ultimate purpose as forming the church *through personal salvation.* Recalling that the Functional View looked like:

God's Ultimate Purpose → Saving People

His Means to that End → Church

The Ontological View looks like:

God's Ultimate Purpose → Forming a People for Himself
His Means to that End → Personal Salvation

In one way, this is only a slight change. After all, Chan has merely swapped means and ends. However, the implications of this slight shift are enormous.

An immediate concern about this view is that it appears to diminish the importance of individual salvation. This is not the case. Personal salvation is still the necessary precondition for being a part of God's people; it is simply not the end in itself. The greater purpose, of which personal salvation is the necessary entryway, is belonging to the people of God.

We suggested previously that the church's connection to God in the Functional View was somewhat arbitrary since God could have chosen to use any means for his purpose. In Chan's Ontological View, the connection is strong and intimate. In this view, the church only exists to the degree that it is united to Christ its head and that its members are held together by the Holy Spirit.

This people of God theme suggests that our God, who is an eternal social unity (Holy Trinity), has intended from before creation to fashion for himself a social unity counterpart to love and from whom to receive love. According to Chan, this is God's great and ultimate purpose in creating. In order to underline the difference in these views, Chan has somewhere observed that the church does not exist to fix the broken world. Instead, the world exists so that God could bring forth his people.

Returning to the earlier question, once someone is saved why do you need the church? The Functional View does not have an answer that many will find motivating. The Ontological

View, on the other hand, is significantly more inspirational. If being a part of God's people is likened to going on a vacation, then personal salvation is the ticket you need to take the trip. Why would a person ever be satisfied with simply possessing his or her ticket and not actually take the trip? Stated another way, more closely related to Scripture, if personal salvation is the necessary entryway to being a part of the people of God, how could a person ever be content with stopping at the doorway? Why would someone not proceed to enter the beautiful thing that God is building for himself?

THE BEAUTY OF BELONGING

Having considered how things have gone wrong, it is time to consider a different perspective. What would it look like if the church was keenly aware of who we are and whose we are? How might things be different if we did not simply acknowledge the obligation of *Belonging to the Community of Faith* but celebrated the incredible privilege that it is? In the next few paragraphs, we will consider the beauty of belonging.

Hesed as belonging

The dictionary definition of the word *belonging* encompasses both the idea of possession and of intimacy in a relationship. When we belong to a group of people, we feel safe and included, and that fosters a willingness to invest. We are empowered to receive and to give in that space. In recent years, especially following the upheaval and isolation of the COVID-19 pandemic, the concept of belonging has garnered more attention. For example, our local public school adopted the motto "Become. Belong. Be Northern." Educators realize that learning happens best when students are connected, not only to the material being taught but also to the other people in the room. Until we feel like we belong, we struggle to thrive: to grow, to take risks, and to bear fruit.

God created us to be connected to him and to one another, and his desire to be attached to us is woven throughout Scripture. When biblical authors wanted to describe the character of God, they often used the Hebrew word *hesed*, which is translated in a variety of ways: great love, faithful love, loving-kindness. *Hesed* is God's loyal, enduring, promise-keeping love. It's what the *Jesus Storybook Bible* calls God's "Never Stopping, Never Giving Up, Unbreaking, Always and Forever Love" for his children.[10] Moses appeals to God's *hesed* when asking for forgiveness for the people of Israel. Ruth shows *hesed* to Naomi in standing by her and declaring, "Where you go, I will go; where you lodge, I will lodge; your people shall be my people, and your God my God" (Ruth 1:16).

In the book *The Other Half of Church*, Jim Wilder and Michel Hendricks describe *hesed* as "relational glue." They write, "Our *hesed* with Jesus is an attachment flowing with life, a strong and permanent bond. Jesus is attached to his Father, and he wants the same with us. He commands us to have the same attachment with each other."[11] The authors describe the difference between "high-*hesed*" environments, where relationships are filled with joy, and "low-*hesed*" environments, where relationships are transactional.[12] We belong to a triune God, who has always existed in community, in a vibrant dance of abundance and delight. His faithful, joyful love is integral to his being and integral to our life together.

Community of faith as a people belonging to God

While we articulate the beauty of this belonging in terms of "the community of faith," an alternative term that may be more inspiring or fruitful is the biblical notion of the people of God. The idea of the people of God is at least *a*, if not *the* fundamental way of understanding God's relationship to humanity. What is sometimes called the "peoplehood formula"—I will be your God, and you will be my people—occurs over fifty times in the Bible, beginning in Genesis and continuing through Revelation.

One of the most moving occurrences of this idea is found in the book of Hosea, where we learn that Hosea's wife Gomer has conceived two children to some other man. The first is called *Lo-ruhamah*, which means "not pitied or loved," and the second is called *Lo-ammi*, which means "not my people." Although these children are the result of and reminders of infidelity, we see God's enormous compassion and grace in his promises that "I will have pity on *Lo-ruhamah*, and I will say to *Lo-ammi*, 'You are my people'; and he shall say, 'You are my God'" (Hosea 2:23).

In the New Testament, the apostle Peter tells the early church: "You are a chosen people, a royal priesthood, a holy nation, God's own people. . . . Once you were not a people, but now you are God's people; once you had not received mercy, but now you have received mercy" (1 Peter 2:9–10 NRSVue). Like the ancient Israelites, we were once *Lo-ruhamah* and *Lo-ammi*, but now we have become the people of God. Like Hosea's children, we are the chosen and forgiven beloved, who belong to God as those grafted into a covenant community.

Cultivating a culture of belonging

If belonging to God means belonging to the people of God, how then shall we live? What do we say about this core value to the unchurched, the casually de-churched, and the de-churched casualties around us? What do we say to those in our midst who feel detached? How can we cultivate cultures of belonging and attachment in our congregations? Here are four ideas for cultivating "high-*hesed*" environments in our church families.

Cultivate a return to Anabaptism. It seems clear that our current plight could be remedied to some degree if we once again focused on the neglected Anabaptist emphases of 1) understanding justification as the starting point of the larger goal of being a disciple, and 2) accepting the covenant community as the indispensable arena for discipleship and, if Simon Chan is right, the actual purpose of creation.

For too long, we have proclaimed the grace of the gospel without the obligations of the gospel and personal salvation without our God-given need for others. Let us return to our Anabaptist roots by living out both the blessed opportunity and the serious expectation of discipleship within a covenant community.

Cultivate joyful dependence. Cultivating a sense of belonging in the community of faith requires more than inclusion—more than simply making room for others. The apostle Paul wrote that "we, who are many, are one body in Christ, and individually we are members one of another" (Romans 12:5). When we say that we belong to the body of Christ, we are declaring: I need you. You need me. We do not have the luxury of giving up on each other, and we are called to a deeper level of commitment to and dependence upon one another.

I (Naomi) remember a time when I was in need and ashamed to ask for help. My small group at church rallied to provide for my needs, but as grateful as I was for the assistance, I struggled to accept it until a friend reframed the situation. She thanked me profusely for giving her the opportunity to take care of me. "This was a gift!" she declared. In a world that celebrates independence, what might it look like to be the kind of people who celebrate dependence? How might we reframe our seasons of weakness and need as opportunities for our church families to love us well? When we claim to be the people of God, we are acknowledging that "in him we live and move and have our being" (Acts 17:28). We are spiritual beings, born of God, transformed by the power of his Son, and completely dependent upon his Spirit. We do not stand alone.

Cultivate authentic relationships. As a fourth-generation pastor, I (Naomi) come from a long line of pastor's kids. That role was ultimately a blessing in my life, but it is not a comfortable thing to live in the spotlight. Growing up, my sisters and I nicknamed the church "our fishbowl" because of the sense of transparency we felt swimming in the waters of our faith community. Yet we were held by those waters and by the prayers and love of the congregation, and my parents were intentional about including us in their ministry and welcoming our honest questions and complaints.

The vulnerability that my parents modeled as leaders, both at home and in the church, is a critical ingredient in a healthy community of faith. As we are aware of the ways that others struggle, we feel safe to share our own struggles. As we build a culture of authenticity, we can be seen and known for who we truly are. Only as we cultivate honesty and trust can we have genuine accountability, the kind that says, "I need you to remind me who I am in Christ." Yes, there is ugliness and brokenness in the church because there is ugliness and brokenness in the human heart. What we celebrate in coming together is not that we are perfect, but that we have tasted and seen the goodness of the God who is at work in our midst (Psalm 34). We celebrate the possibility of redemption, healing, and hope, even for sinners like us.

Cultivate generational connections. After dinner one night, I (Naomi) asked my family, "Why do you go to church?" For my small daughter, it is the pleasure of dressing up and seeing her friends. For my son, it is a place where he feels comfortable and at home. For my tall daughter, it is the joy of beautiful music and learning to sing parts with the congregation. For my husband, it is the gift of other believers whose faith will buoy him in times of doubt or discouragement. As we move through seasons of life, our needs change, and what we can give and receive in the community of faith will also change. But every generation needs spaces in the church to be known and in which to serve, and ideally those needs are met in shared ways.

Christina Embree helps churches foster discipleship across generations, and she explains that the six living generations have unique gifts and needs that they bring into the community of faith.[13] To use my own family as an example: My parents are Baby Boomers who bring a strong work ethic, knowledge, and experience to the table. They need a place to pass on their faith and a way to leave a legacy. My husband and I are Millennials who bring a deep desire for mentorship, community, and authentic faith and practice. We need a role to fill and a place to belong in the church family. My children are members of Generation Z with gifts of technological fortitude, a global worldview, and an orientation toward justice. They need a place to discover who they are and to have opportunities to grow and fail. When our churches are safe places where generational needs can be met, we foster lifelong discipleship, because a sense of belonging in the community of faith is critical to our continuation in the faith.

A SYMPHONY OF PRAISE

After Jesus instructed his disciples on what to do when a brother or sister sins against them, he said this: "Truly I tell you, whatever you bind on earth will be bound in heaven, and whatever you loose on earth will be loosed in heaven. Again, truly I tell you, if two of you agree on earth about anything you ask, it will be done for you by my Father in heaven. For where two or three are gathered in my name, I am there among them" (Matthew 18:18–20). The word that Jesus uses for "agree" is *sumphoneo*, which means "sound together" and from which we get the word "symphony."

Something extraordinary happens when a single musician joins a symphony, when she adds her music to the music of others—it is a fuller, richer sound. So it is in the community of faith. Connecting with God as individuals is important for spiritual formation, but the extraordinary happens as the body of Christ gathers. As we play our music together, we experience a fuller manifestation of the body of Christ than we can experience on our own. To return to the words of Peter: "You are a chosen people, a royal priesthood, a holy nation, God's own people, in order that you may proclaim the excellence of him who called you out of darkness into his marvelous light" (1 Peter 2:9 NRSVue). As we live out our calling to be the covenant community, a people belonging to God, we become a symphony of praise. We proclaim his mighty acts and witness to the wonder of his marvelous light in our lives.

• • • • • • • • • • • • • • • • • •

RESPONSE ESSAY

Belonging to the Community of Faith

▶ *Santiago Espitia Fajardo, Bogotá, Colombia*

My community is in the capital city of Bogotá, Colombia. Bogotá is a large city with approximately eight million inhabitants, and Catholicism is the dominant religion of the Colombian population in generational groups between eighteen and sixty-one years old or older, representing about 57 percent of the population. A significant number, nearly 22 percent, of believers are Protestant.[14] In Colombia there are many megachurches. Certain aspects of this church model attract people. One aspect is an emphasis on spirituality at the individual level, which goes hand-in-hand with an emphasis on the importance of "always feeling good." In these churches there is little or no community responsibility. The emphasis on an individualized spirituality means that the *other* does not interest or worry me.

Because these churches embrace a Functional View, as described in the essay, it limits their ability to build community and talking about "belonging to community" is a challenge.

In contrast, my church is a small community of no more than fifty members in which we all know one other. In our faith community we seek to strengthen meaningful relational ties with one another. Our community is held together not only based on what we believe, but also on what we live. Knowing one another helps us take care of one another.

BIC Colombia shares in the challenge presented in the essay, showing that as Christians in the Western world, we currently find ourselves in a situation where *Belonging to the Community of Faith* is not understood as an aspect necessary for the

Christian life. In Colombia, many people of faith consider that they do not need the church because it seems irrelevant to their lives. This is because the church has often overemphasized the religious aspect but has not transcended it to the level of real, felt needs. Therefore, it is common for people to find in other spaces (communities) what the church does not offer them.

MORE THAN RELIGION

The Anabaptists of the sixteenth century understood that belonging to the community of faith was an essential part of life. Community was not a limited aspect of life, rather the ecclesiology was understood from the political, economic, and social challenges that being neither Protestant nor Catholic implied. Against this historical backdrop, we today must also understand that being part of the church is much more than a religious matter.

In this sense, it is necessary for the church to understand that it is part of society, and therefore it must be relevant and pertinent to it. The first communities that followed Jesus followed him in life: in all aspects, economic, social, ethical, and political. Today, it is necessary for the church in Colombia and the world to also understand this, that following Jesus implies following him in life. It is a matter of changing one's worldview; as the apostle Paul would say, "Change your way of thinking, so that your way of living changes" (Romans 12:1–2 author translation).

CHALLENGES TO COMMUNITY

The church in Latin America has nuances and challenges to fostering Christlike community specific to the region; for example: high economic inequality, low levels of education, forced migration, and violence. These and other realities mean that understanding what it means to belong to a community of faith has other implications and challenges.

The report titled "Social Panorama of Latin America"[15] shows that societies facing great uncertainty experience a persistence of inequality. Further, intersecting inequalities increase the risk of falling deeper into poverty due to the loss of labor income. Poverty is one of the main obstacles to achieving sustainable development in Latin America. Unemployment is also a major problem in our region, mainly affecting young people and people with low levels of education. According to recent data, the unemployment rate across Latin America is approximately 8 percent, generating great economic and social instability.

Low levels of education are a relevant problem in our region. Approximately a quarter of the Latin American population does not have access to quality education. This is due to various factors, such as lack of infrastructure, insufficient investment in educational programs, and inequality in access to educational opportunities.

Forced migrations affect many Latin American countries. People leave their homes due to armed conflict, political persecution, gang violence, and situations of extreme poverty. According to recent figures, nearly four and a half million people have left their countries in search of safety and better living conditions.

Unfortunately, Latin America faces high levels of violence in different forms, such as gender violence, urban violence, and violence related to organized crime. These pressures have a significant impact on people's safety and peaceful coexistence in our societies. Violence in Colombia, specifically, transcends the individual and impacts entire communities, jeopardizing the quality of life for everyone. All armed actors have incorporated the attack on the civilian population as a war strategy. However, the modalities of violence used and the intensity of their actions differ according to the evaluations that each actor makes of the territory, the moment of the war, and the strategies they deploy, within which the civilian population is involved.

Communities of faith have not been exempted from these manifestations of conflict and violence. Churches have suffered the impacts of conflict in different ways: murder of their leaders—priests, pastors, nuns—and members of their communities, forced displacement, stigmatization, and attacks against sacred places, among other forms of violence. Amid all of the violence, faith communities have shown that faith and spirituality experienced by and in the community help, not only to embrace nonviolence, but to overcome and even transform the damage caused by war and violence.[16] This is the hope we carry, that the church upholds people of faith amid these challenges.

. . . .

RESPONSE ESSAY

Belonging to the Community of Faith

▶ *Brian Ross, Fresno, California*

As a seminary professor, most of my students live with the tension of being called by the Spirit to serve in ministry, while acknowledging that fewer and fewer of their contemporaries have interest in the church. I have often been asked, "What would you say to someone who asked you why they should belong to a church?"

LONGING FOR FREEDOM

Most of us have experienced a nagging sense that we do not always have our own best interest in mind. When we simply live according to what seems to make most sense to us, we often unintentionally cause ourselves and others real problems. Self-destructive addictions. Relational patterns that do not end well. Making decisions that rarely turn out as we hoped. Paul gives language to this common experience: "I do not do the good I want to do, but the evil I do not want to do—this I keep on doing" (Romans 7:19 NIV).

Even though we desire to be free to live as we think is best, we are not nearly as free as we often believe. We are prisoners of our own biological desires and are much more shaped by the will of the rich and powerful than we acknowledge. Algorithms and marketing campaigns are designed to shape our loves in ways that we often cannot fully comprehend. Historian Yuval Harari names this common condition:

> You have this fantasy, that you. . . just choose whatever you want freely. . . . In reality, many of our choices, our desires,

they are influenced by cultural factors, political campaigns of propaganda, by biological processes in our body.[17]

This is the human predicament.

Historically speaking, the earliest Christians did not view salvation as one-sided, as merely experiencing divine forgiveness, but as being saved from our own natural, innate, destructive patterns. Salvation is the experience of being delivered from our own ways and being freed to live aligned with the values and patterns of Jesus of Nazareth. Paul again writes, "We. . . are being transformed into his image" (2 Corinthians 3:18 NIV). And St. Irenaeus, in the early second century, echoes the same: "Our Lord Jesus Christ. . . did, through his transcendent love, become what we are, that he might bring us to be even what he is himself."[18] Church is intended to be the spiritual community in whom our active participation forms us into the ways of Jesus.

TAKING ON THE CHARACTER OF JESUS

The fourth century BC Greek philosopher Aristotle has had a profound impact on the Christian church. He noted that to experience life-change requires proper concepts and experiential habits.

> Virtue of thought arises and grows mainly from teaching; that is why it needs experience and time. Virtue of character results from habit.[19]

But why does this take a community? Could not the dedicated spiritual seeker simply apply themselves to learning from Jesus without a church? Human beings are social creatures. What we believe, or even live, all on our own, quickly begins to feel like private fantasy. Our conception of reality requires a community to confirm it deep within our psyche. Charles Taylor refers to this as a "social imaginary":

> "By social imaginary. . . I am thinking. . . of the ways people. . . fit together with others, how things go on between them. . . the deeper normative notions. . . that underlie these expectations. . . .The way ordinary people "imagine" their surroundings. . . carried in images, stories, and legends. . . . Theory is often the possession of a small minority. . . the social imaginary is shared by large groups of people."[20]

In effect we catch, through the Spirit, new patterns of life as we actively participate and experience a different type of social arrangement. If I recognize that I need a newer and better way to live, if I recognize that my natural life (my normal way), tends to warp me and hurt others, and if I am genuinely open to becoming a different kind of person in the manner of Jesus, I need to regularly engage a community of faith to be formed in the Way (Colossians 3:1–16).

Too many mainstream churches have other goals, besides becoming like Jesus, as their lived mission. There may not be much to hope for the Christian future if our churches merely operate with the same goals as other 501(c)(3) organizations.

The BIC are right to value *Belonging to the Community of Faith*. By cultivating a Jesus culture of belonging, we offer a context where others can become like him. The best of the BIC has always had the aim to imitate Jesus. If this is our goal, active participation in a church is. . . everything.

. . . .

CHAPTER 5

Discussion Questions

1. In what ways might we continually remind ourselves of and practice the corporate dimension of the faith?
2. How might our discipleship efforts look different if we genuinely emphasized belonging to a community of faith as a fundamental precondition of the Christian life?
3. Does your experience of church more closely reflect Chan's Functional View or Ontological View? What markers indicate this for you?
4. How have you experienced God's *hesed*, his loyal love? When and where have you felt a sense of belonging and attachment to the body of Christ?
5. What might it look like to cultivate joyful dependence, authentic relationships, and generational connections in our communities of faith?

CHAPTER 6

Witnessing to the World

Erica and Jonathan Lloyd

We value an active and loving witness for Christ to all people.

INTRODUCTION

The BIC statement regarding our witness to the world has not always accurately characterized our denomination, but today it is an important part of how we engage the world around us, both corporately and individually. Our core values start with a firm foundation of knowing Jesus and being in relationship with him. We know about him through the Scriptures and walk out our faith in community. We are committed to a witness that comes from love, knows that the love of God is good for everyone, and endures challenges. With this in place, our core value of "an active and loving witness for Christ to all people" provides an encouraging, purposeful, and joy-filled approach to putting our relationship with Jesus into action in the world around us.[1]

In the early days of our BIC history, we focused on how our daily lives reflected holiness and obedience in practical and sometimes externally obvious ways, such as a plain form of clothing. We put a high value on being a community, separated from the world around us. We assumed that those who were intrigued by our way of life would come and ask us about it, providing opportunities for witnessing.[2]

In the midst of significant societal change following the Civil War, we experienced shifts in our approach to witnessing. We were learning from other Jesus followers as they developed various forms of outreach and service,[3] and we became convinced that Jesus' famous words in "Go therefore and make disciples of all nations. . ." (Matthew 28:19) sounded more active than our practice of focusing on the boundaries of holiness and obedience in our own lives and hoping people would want to join in. Between 1890 and 1910 BIC launched city mission outreach efforts in urban centers like Chicago, Des Moines, Buffalo, and Philadelphia.[4] During this same time we began to send international missionaries first to southern Africa and shortly thereafter to India. Church planting and evangelism efforts in our local communities as well as internationally led to a period of church growth for the BIC in the twentieth century, and continues as a significant part of how we, as BIC, seek to live and act in the world today.

FOUNDATIONS FOR *WITNESSING TO THE WORLD*

Witnessing to the World builds upon several other core values. Without *Experiencing God's Love and Grace*, we have nothing about which we can witness. If we do not *Believe the Bible* or haven't decided to *Follow Jesus*, there is no good reason to love others in the selfless way necessary to be an active and loving witness. In addition, effective witnessing is a group activity. We need to value *Belonging to a Community of Faith* enough to actually do it, even when it is difficult or discouraging, in order that we can effectively witness and then disciple new believers. These four core values are essential foundation pieces of our loving and active witness for Christ.

Several additional experiences or convictions are needed. First, we need to respond to our experience of God's love and grace by loving God in return. This loving relationship is what makes it possible for people to do difficult things with great joy, and we live in a world where doing difficult things with great joy is like a light shining in a dark place. The apostles often experienced miraculous healings as accompaniments to their spoken witness (Acts 3:1–8, 5:12, 8:4–8, etc.), but their joy and patience in the face of difficulties was another miraculous testimony that confirmed their words about the good news of Jesus.

In addition, we must experience our own relationship with and acceptance by God as something so precious and valuable that we know it will be precious and valuable to others if they experience it. For Jesus to say that he and the Father are one (John 10:30) was a startling and controversial statement. If it were not true, it would have been the greatest arrogance. But it is true. For us to say that we know the way to God and the best way to live is similarly arrogant—unless we really do. Western society has largely accepted that everyone will have the best life if they discern, determine, and live out their own individual truths. We are unlikely to witness for Christ in this environment until we know through experience that following him is the unique path to true life, resilient joy, and eternal blessings. Living out our core value of witnessing in our world today means we start by asking ourselves if we have really experienced this, and if we have not, we become like the persistent widow (Luke 18:1–8), or the nighttime visitor banging on the door (Luke 11:5–8), asking, seeking, knocking until we do experience it (Luke 11:9). When we have experienced God's love as something everyone would want if they knew how good it was, witnessing can be a joyful opportunity rather than a heavy obligation.

Witnessing to the World also requires that we know that our relationship with God is like the treasure hidden in the field—worth selling or losing everything else to be able to attain (Matthew 13:44). In many parts of the world, choosing to follow Jesus is a dangerous decision. In a majority of the world, it is an unpopular decision. We believe that all people should hear about Jesus in an understandable way and be invited to follow him. We therefore need to believe that following Jesus is worth the danger, to those who carry the message and also to those who receive it. We remember the words of Peter, when Jesus asked the disciples if they also wanted to leave him because following was getting difficult. Peter replied, "'Lord, to whom can we go? You have the words of eternal life. We have come to believe and know that you are the Holy One of God" (John 6:68–69). In Hebrews, scripture says that the pain of the cross was worth it to Jesus because of the joy he would have when he had saved us (Hebrews 12:2). That is a lot of joy. We can follow that example, and focus on the joy of following Jesus, even when it involves suffering.

Experiencing God's Love and Grace, Believing the Bible, Following Jesus, and *Belonging to a Community of Faith* are BIC core values that fuel an active and loving witness to the world. We cannot see effective witnessing when these other values are neglected. Furthermore, each one of these values or convictions leads to the strengthening of the others. As we live them out, we are empowered to act with purpose and joy in relation to the world around us.

AN ACTIVE AND LOVING WITNESS FOR CHRIST TO ALL PEOPLE

With these foundational values and convictions in place, we can turn our attention to understanding what an active and loving witness for Christ to all people looks like and how it causes us to live. The wording of this core value is significant. The word *witness* is different from the word *evangelize* in some distinct ways that give guidance to our approach. All of the descriptive words related to witness are also important. *Active*, *loving*, *for Christ*, and *to all people* matter when we consider our relationships with the people around us to whom we desire to be a witness.

Witness vs. evangelize

As we developed our core values, it would have been possible to use the word *evangelize* instead of *witness*. *Evangelize* means to preach the gospel or seek to convert someone to Christianity. This is not a bad word, and we do both of those things as BIC people. However, our historic understanding of the importance of obedient discipleship and belonging to a community means that we hesitate to put too much emphasis on moments of conversion or adopt evangelism practices focused on obtaining them.[5] *Witness*, on the other hand, means the attestation of a fact or event, one who has personal knowledge of something, or one who gives evidence. Witnesses share their experiences; they embrace a posture that recognizes that their sharing may lead to a response from the listener. Using the word *witness* helps us remember that we do not have the responsibility or the power to cause our listeners to choose to follow Jesus; in other words, we cannot control the outcome. We focus, instead, on sharing our experiences of the love and grace of God and freedom found in Jesus.

Active witness

In our role as witnesses, our focus on sharing rather than response does not mean that we approach witnessing entirely as we did in the early days of the BIC. We do not live our lives with our church friends and run our church programs and hope someone asks to know about Jesus. The city missions, revival services, and cross-cultural missionary efforts begun in the late 1800s were some initial steps in our commitment to value an *active* witness. Even with our increased activity, we discovered that our commitment to maintain a visibly separate Christian community, expressed primarily through wearing plain clothing, established barriers that made it difficult for people to want to join.[6] We no longer have an established or even an informal dress code for BIC people, but our desire to be active witnesses requires us to discern what barriers exist between us and the people we are hoping to witness to.

A church is an intimidating place for people who do not yet belong to it. And in places where believers need to meet secretly, the "We hope you come and join us" approach to witnessing is simply not effective. In these settings, personal, intentional, and careful witnessing creates a way for people to come to know Jesus.

If we have a heartfelt desire that others would come to know and experience the love and grace of God, we must be intentional and active in seeking out ways to make him known to them outside of our church buildings and its programs. This means that we, as a group, need to spend some of our time, attention, and resources being witnesses outside of the church building. It also means that as individual BIC members, we can choose to participate actively in sharing God's love broadly outside our church families. A number of American

BIC church buildings are used throughout the week by organizations that meet needs in the community, and members of those churches serve in various community organizations outside the BIC church. Resources of time and facilities that could be focused on making the church programs better are instead given to being a witness in the community at large. This is an active and intentional allocation of resources to witnessing and involves both the church acting together and people making individual choices to be witnesses.

An active witness is an encouraging value in today's world. There are seemingly unsolvable challenges and injustices all around us. We do not know how to change these things that are too big for us. Though many organizations and individuals are working diligently to help solve problems and bring change to societies, it does not take much life experience to discover that our best attempts to fix things often go astray through sinful actions or unintended negative consequences.

The good news is that Jesus promised to go with us as we witness for him in this chaotic, violent, and unjust world (Matthew 28:20). When we feel powerless to change anything about the evil in our world, it is encouraging to remember that Jesus entrusted a handful of largely uneducated minority people in the most powerful nation that existed at that time to be witnesses. The disciples' active witness to the death and resurrection of Jesus, combined with their active service to the poor, and the miraculous healing power of Jesus did eventually bring significant changes that still impact the world today. Though we may be surrounded by unsolvable problems and unspeakable evils, we need not succumb to helplessness and hopelessness. It is encouraging to know that our active witness gives us a valuable contribution despite our surroundings.

Loving witness

Throughout the history of the church, different approaches to witnessing and missions have attempted to spread the gospel message. There have been many genuine faithful witnesses, but there were also sinful attitudes and practices, when converting people became unhelpfully prioritized over loving them. As the BIC, we value a loving witness, which comes from a posture of the heart that wants good things for other people. It accepts the reality that some people will be offended by the message of Jesus. However, a loving witness avoids or removes unnecessary stumbling blocks in someone's path toward Jesus. While being a loving witness will not guarantee that people will like us or accept our message, it will give the best possible chance for them to understand Jesus' love and choose to accept his grace.

We love God, and we are growing to want the things God wants, so we love people and want them to be saved (1 Timothy 2:4). We share about the love and grace of God and witness to God's redemption in our lives because we hope that others will experience those things as well. Our motivation sometimes becomes evident when people become new followers of Jesus. If our first concern is that they come to our BIC church, agree with our BIC doctrine, or begin to talk and act like good BIC church people, we might not be primarily motivated by a loving desire for them to experience the love of God that we have experienced. We witness out of love, and we seek God's best for the people that we witness to, even if it looks different than God's best for us.

When we are loving witnesses, with love for God and love for others as the motivation, we do not want people to get stuck at roadblocks on their way to relationship with Jesus. We are honest, however, about the fact that the good message of Jesus' saving grace for sinful people can be offensive, for various reasons. Paul says that we can give a bad odor to those who have rejected the way of salvation, even when we are a life-giving aroma to those who are following the way of Jesus (2 Corinthians 2:15–16). It seems Paul even expresses the pain of this reality when he says, "Who is sufficient for these things?" Paul is not talking here about the aroma of people who are being bad witnesses. He is saying that the way of Jesus is not good news to everyone. A witness testifies to what they have seen and experienced. If we have experienced our need for, and God's provision of, forgiveness for our sins, and the grace and love of God, that is the message for our witnessing. If we change the message because we think (or know) that it will be offensive to some people, we are no longer loving witnesses, because in this message is the way to eternal life. Loving witnesses accept that some will be offended, but they remain committed to truthfully proclaiming the message.

A loving witness is very careful not to add offenses to the already challenging message of Jesus that might make it more difficult for people to accept. We do not want our preferences, our cultural norms, or our methodology to become an unnecessary hindrance between Jesus and the people with whom we want to share the good news. Our first BIC missionaries to Zimbabwe were accepted by the Matabele people in the Matopo Hills partly because they showed love by adapting to a local diet and joining in the work their neighbors were doing.[7] However, we do not have to go across a national or cultural barrier for this to apply. Our attitudes and words toward people either pave the way for a communication of the good news of Jesus or set up barriers. Understanding the difference between the necessary offense of the gospel message and unnecessary stumbling blocks takes wisdom and humility.

Being a loving witness is a joyful value in today's world. Jesus warned his disciples that the love of many would grow cold (Matthew 24:12). We do not have to look very far to see this principle in action. I am grateful that God gives us the mission of being loving witnesses. It does not have to be expensive (although it might be), it does not have to take hours (although it could), and there are ways to love that suit every personality type and every gifting given to people in the body of Christ. People generally respond well to being loved. Although it can be a lot of work, it can also be a lot of fun! Into darkness, discouragement, fear, and all manner of oppressive things, we get to show up—not with a responsibility to understand and fix everything, but with the call to be a loving witness.

Witness for Christ

We value a witness for Christ. Although we can witness for Christ through tangible works like providing good medical care, giving financially through nonprofit organizations that do good community work, donating to local food pantries, or engaging in social justice activism, we do not imply or believe that these things are the end goal of our witness. While these can be wonderful forms of "active and loving witness," we are not witnesses *for* them, because they do not have the gift of eternal life. We value a witness for Christ, because the power, forgiveness, and love of Christ is what we have experienced to be transformational. All our loving actions and service in our communities is a gift we are giving because of Jesus and on behalf of Jesus. We are therefore God's ambassadors, as though God were making his appeal through us (2 Corinthians 5:20). Our good works are freely given, without expecting anything in return, but we always remember that we are freely giving them as a picture and a signpost to the grace and forgiveness Jesus has given us and that he wants to give to others.

Being a witness for Christ is a vision-giving word in today's world, at all times throughout history, and also into the future. Jesus is amazing, God's mercy is so vast that it is almost unbelievable, and Holy Spirit's presence and power are indescribably comforting. Nothing else that we can be excited about in terms of good news can even come close to this. Regardless of what catastrophe comes to pass, God will still be all-powerful and completely good. Jesus will still be waiting for us on the other side of the grave, and Holy Spirit will still accompany us every step of the way. This is the best story ever. When, in an exhortation to not grow weary following Jesus, the writer of Hebrews tells us to "[fix] our eyes on Jesus" (Hebrews 12:2 NIV), he was telling us how to maintain vision in the midst of hardship. The way to have joy, resilience, and hope in the world today is to remain focused on Christ. Being a witness for Christ means that we get to share this effective and incredible vision with others.

Witness to all people

We value a witness to all people. The BIC wants all people to receive the good message in a language they can understand, and with as few unnecessary stumbling blocks as possible. This value of a witness to all people comes with a very large number: eight billion people. These eight billion people live in approximately 17,428 unique people groups. A people group is a group with a common language and culture. If enough people in a specific people group become followers of Jesus, there are enough of them to provide the witness to the rest of their group. If a people group does not consist of 2 percent Jesus followers, it cannot be expected that the members of that people group will have a chance to hear the witness about Jesus, unless someone from outside their group shares it with them. In the world as of this writing, 7,382 people groups (3.4 billion individual people) still lack that threshold of 2 percent Jesus followers, and they are referred to as unreached people groups.[8]

As a body, we support the work of witnessing by our brothers and sisters in the places to which God gifts and calls them. Because there are still many unreached people groups, we will make sure that some of our collective effort, enthusiasm, prayers, and financial resources remain directed toward getting the witness of Christ to them, since someone from outside their group has to go in for them to have a witness. We will do this through sending missionaries, sending resources, interceding, and working in partnership with Christian brothers and sisters from other church backgrounds, so that the witness about Jesus can reach all people.

Witnessing to all people is an exciting value in today's world. When we look at the marvelous diversity of everything from landscapes to vegetation and animal life, we get a glimpse into the incredible creativity of God. It is similar with people groups. God is more clearly seen in the many languages, cultures, customs, and beautiful physical diversity of his people than he could ever be in any one of them. Far from witnessing to all people in order to make them culturally more like us, we witness to all people and marvel at how God leads and guides them to worship him in ways that are uniquely suited to their cultures and languages. God is seen to be as big as he really is when we see him made visible in many cultures and languages.

CONCLUSION

One of the great joys of the Christian life is helping someone else become a part of God's family. Witnessing is the first step in this. Our core value: *an active and loving witness for Christ to all people* gives us a place to start and ways to grow as we follow Jesus in the area of witnessing.

We have experienced the love and grace of God, so we have something to bear witness to. Starting even with our fellow believers, we can become comfortable talking about what God has done for us or is doing in our lives. When this kind of talking becomes natural for us, we will be more likely to witness to those who are not yet believers. As churches, we can celebrate with those who share stories of God's goodness and encourage each other to see his love and faithfulness at work.

We can actively look for opportunities for witness in the world around us. God's creativity in finding avenues for us to witness is available as we become committed to looking for them. If we realize that we spend almost all our time with Christian people, we can choose a hobby or a volunteer role that will allow us to spend time with people who do not yet know Jesus. We can begin to pray regularly for opportunities to share God's love with our coworkers. We can choose to use some of our church budgets to give to our local community or support a missionary. Far from being complicated, being an active witness is largely a matter of focus and intention.

We can grow in being a loving witness. American culture says that loving someone implies agreement and affirmation—disagree or choose not to affirm, and you are likely to be labeled unloving. Fortunately, we don't have to convince people we are loving, we can live it out. We can seek ways to show love that are unmistakable for anything else—where we get nothing in return yet continue to do loving actions. As Christians, we can help each other love those outside the church by loving one another well inside the church, even in the midst of differences and disagreements.

"A body, though one, has many parts" (1 Corinthians 12:12 NIV). Paul's metaphor of the body of Christ is useful in many ways, and one of them is when we think about our witness to all people. We are not all local church planters, yet we participate in local church planting when we are part of the body as it participates in local church planting. We work in different kinds of workplaces, but when we witness for Christ in our workplaces, we participate in each other's witnessing because we are part of the body. We are not all cross-cultural missionaries, but when we are part of the body, we participate in the work of cross-cultural missionaries. The witness of the church to all people requires all of us.

The great commission, "Go and make disciples of all nations," (Matthew 28:19 NIV), was never intended to apply to only some of the people who follow Jesus. Our value of *Witnessing to the World* is not a core value just for professional ministers. Jesus said, "The harvest is plentiful but the workers are few. Ask the Lord of the harvest, therefore, to send out workers into his harvest field" (Matthew 9:37–38 NIV). As we all make active, loving witness for Christ one of our core values, we can be part of the harvest Jesus talks about and experience the joy of helping others become followers of Jesus.

· · · · · · · · · · · · · · · · · ·

RESPONSE ESSAY
Witnessing to the World

▶ *David Miller, Quebec, Canada*

As I reflect on the value of *Witnessing to the World* from the perspective of the Quebec context, it is both a sobering and stimulating experience. Quebec, with a population of about 8.7 million people, has a very low percentage of people who are living as followers of Christ. In this way, Quebec resembles Spain, a sister context in which the BIC has sought to faithfully witness to the good news of Christ since the 1980s. The challenges of seeking to witness in Quebec include an indifference to any talk about God combined with an image of church (in any expression) as an undesirable piece of the past that Quebec society is leaving behind. This is truly sobering and, at times, daunting.

Quebec is also a stimulating place to live and to engage in witnessing for Christ. We live and serve in this place where over 75 percent of the population speak French as their first language. This francophone reality combines with a culture that values humor and authenticity in relationships. Creativity and resourcefulness abound in this northern land, where snow beautifully defines the landscape during at least four months of the year. Living and witnessing moves us to thank God for his grace expressed in this remarkable culture and to see the importance of prayer that Christ would be known through the impact of each believer and of every church, small or large.

ACTIVE AND LOVING WITNESS IN QUEBEC
Accenting a witness as active and loving connects well with my context. Speaking of witness in this way ties it closely

to the way that we are living our lives with God, with one another, and in the world. God's gracious and transforming work in our lives moves to the center of what it means to be able to witness. This living expression of witness opens the way for the sharing of "an accounting for the hope that is in you" (1 Peter 3:15). Without some kind of demonstration of the reality of reconciliation, hope, and love in our lives, there is rarely any interest in a message concerning God or a life of faith in God. Rather than speaking of witness as either focusing on life example or on the spoken word, in Quebec there is a real sense in which the Spirit's work in our lives is significant in communicating the good news of Jesus.

Because of this, strengthening our witness in Quebec is closely linked to discipleship. In our individual experiences and in our life as the church, are we growing as people who know Christ and who desire to make him known? If so, a sense of joy and mission will take root. We can remind one another that our witness does not depend on a particular program, but on the transformation of hearts that are turning toward sharing the good news with those around us, rather than being driven by our own personal projects and desires. In this way, we can discover more and more what is means to let our light shine before those around us (Matthew 5:16). In Quebec, linking witness and discipleship can build a strong and long-lasting witness in this place with minimal Christian presence.

This experience of witness, as a result of transformed lives, is a true break in approach from seeing witness for Christ primarily as an obligation. In the religious history of Quebec, faithfulness to God was framed for many years as simply doing what the Catholic Church expected of you. While this guilt-driven program can surely bring about efforts to do what should be done, it does not result in witness that points to the reality of the love, hope, and forgiveness that we know in Christ. In contrast, witness rooted in freedom, not shame, allows for the full expression of the love of God and of the truth that is in Christ.

EXPRESSIONS OF OUR WITNESS

It is evident in the biblical message and in our experience that our witness is to be Spirit-empowered. One current leader in our network of churches first came into a Sunday time of worship while shopping for a new coat! The sales area was right beside the room that the church rented on Sunday mornings. Curious, she walked into the worship service not knowing that she had come into a church gathering. She was welcomed and God's Spirit worked in her life to bring restoration and life in Christ. She is now a leader in this community of believers.

Weekly home groups that are focused on encouragement and love have been a significant part of witness in Quebec. These groups are open to anyone who would like to come. People with no faith in Christ or who have been living far from God have experienced God's love and heard the word of hope in Christ in these simple gatherings.

As a church, we take time to serve in support of community organizations. Building relationships over years with the leaders of these community groups has led to new possibilities for witness. One of these leaders, glad for the help received with painting and yardwork, asked if I would tell him about what brought me to faith in Christ.

A last expression is the importance of collaboration in witness and in service among believers from different church families. For churches in Quebec, with so little hope and relatively few resources, praying for one another and finding ways to strengthen our common witness are expressions of the desire to faithfully engage in an *active* and *loving* witness for Christ.

We thank God for the ways in which the BIC have been able to share in witness for Christ—an active and loving witness—for over four decades in Quebec. May many more people here come to know the love and truth of the good news of Jesus.

· · · · · · · · · · · · · · · · ·

RESPONSE ESSAY

Witnessing to the World

▶ *Bijoy Roul,*[9] *Odisha, India*

When the BIC became convinced that the great commission of Jesus: "Go therefore and make disciples of all nations. . ." (Matthew 28:19–20) was actually for them too, and when they realized that going and making was much more active than it was passive, they began sending missionaries to the nations. The 1903 BIC General Conference approved a decision to establish a mission point in India, and the first BIC missionaries set sail for Bombay in January 1905. The work was hard, and it was not until 1913 that the mission became established in North Bihar, a state in the northeast region of India.

India is a large country with a huge population. Current estimates are that the population exceeds 1.4 billion people and represents 2,279 different people groups. Approximately 90 percent of the people groups, representing around 95 percent of the population, are unreached with the gospel of Jesus. In my home state of Odisha (formerly known as Orissa) there are almost 51 million people in over 700 people groups. Over 660 people groups in Odisha are classed as unreached because less than 2 percent of the population is Christian.

BIBLICAL FOUNDATION FOR WITNESSING

We believe the great commission is God's mandate for all believers and not something optional or special for only some. God wants the church to grow, and he calls all of us to be part of his work in this world. Jesus came to seek and to save the lost and God is pleased when churches grow in numbers. The

Bible states that there is rejoicing in heaven over every sinner who repents.

Jesus promised his disciples that they would receive power to be witnesses. He said, "You will receive power when the Holy Spirit has come upon you; and you will be my witnesses in Jerusalem, in all Judea and Samaria, and to the ends of the earth" (Acts 1:8). We believe this promise and so we want to be an active witness to the millions of people in Odisha. The Bible also makes clear that Christians are not promised that everything will be beautiful or easy in life. Jesus said that his followers would suffer for the sake of the gospel. In many parts of India, including Odisha, there is much opposition and persecution against Christians. It is very hard and diffi-cult work to be active and loving witnesses for Christ when you know this might bring persecution. For some believers in Odisha, their families will reject them and even cast them out of their village.

AN EFFECTIVE WITNESS

The desire to be an effective witness must begin with prayer. Prayer is not just asking God to bless us and help us in the problems of life. Prayer is seeking to be identified with God in his purposes. When we witness and do evangelism, we are cooperating with him. Through prayer and faith we have seen God work miracles of healing and this has helped to make our witness effective.

The great number of unreached people in Odisha is a heavy burden on my heart. To reach more people we need to train leaders in evangelism and church planting. So BIC Odisha developed plans for witness and multiplication. These plans included current churches looking beyond their local setting and seeing the great need to reach out to more people. They train their people to go out and plant new churches. In this way, the church will multiply and grow. We teach believers how to witness to the different types of people in our towns and villages: Hindus, animists, Muslims, and other tribal people. This includes understanding the beliefs of those we are trying to reach, communicating with people in their own language, and being careful and respectful with our words, concepts, and terminology. We teach the importance of being humble, but also to explain carefully and boldly who Jesus is and God's plan of salvation.

When people come to faith in Jesus, we help them to become part of a church so that they can be nurtured. Our church leaders participate in leadership development programs so that they are ready to receive and nurture new believers. The churches also have programs of leadership development so that new workers are trained. These new workers are encouraged to witness and evangelize and reach new people in other villages. When new people are reached, the whole process starts over again. In this way we have seen many new churches planted.

Another way that we try to be an active and loving witness is through social development for village welfare. We know that God loves people and has a great concern for their welfare and development. Most people in India live in villages and there is a large gap between poor people and rich people. Odisha is known as one of the poorest states in India. Many people have very little food, no electricity, no clean drinking water, no medical or educational facilities. Even though the BIC church in Odisha is poor, we have been trying to help people with their social needs. Our programs have included medical and hygiene programs, educational opportunities for children and adults, vocational training, relief work, and Christian teaching on moral issues related to marriage and alcohol.

With God's help and through prayer, these programs have helped the BIC in Odisha to be an active and loving witness for Christ. We hope the BIC in other countries will be encouraged to work and pray so that they can be active and loving witnesses for Christ in their communities.

. . . .
CHAPTER 6

Discussion Questions

1. What has been your experience with the value of *Witnessing to the World* in your BIC church? Is it encouraged, and if so, how?

2. Is *Witnessing to the World* challenging for you? If so, why do you think that might be? Do you agree or disagree that this value is necessary, and why?

3. Identify the types of resources you use (time, money, skills) to intentionally be an *active* witness.

4. Are there moments when we are a less-than-loving witness? What encouragement do you find in these essays to help you position your heart as a *loving* witness?

5. Considering your personal relationships and your involvement in your community, how are you being called to be a witness to the people around you?

Serving Compassionately

Lynda Gephart and Hank Johnson

> *We value serving others at their point of need,*
> *following the example of our Lord Jesus.*

INTRODUCTION

As BIC seek to embrace the core value of *Serving Compassionately*, and because we strive to live and love like Jesus, we "value serving others at their point of need, following the example of our Lord Jesus."[1]

Jesus' example, portrayed throughout the gospels, motivates and guides our choices as we interact with others, learn about needs, and steward our resources. The witness and the writings of the early church further spur us on, calling us to address needs in our homes, our churches, our schools, our workplaces, our communities, our country, and across the globe. And examples from our BIC predecessors also inspire us today to continue in the long tradition of devoting ourselves to exemplifying the compassion of Christ.

BIC leadership identified the need for an international church emblem in the 1970s, artistically depicting the most significant traits of our denomination: salvation through

Christ (the cross); empowerment by the Holy Spirit, as well as peacemaking (the dove); and humble service (the basin and towel).[2] Serving others has clearly been a major emphasis of being disciples of Jesus throughout our church's history. Just as Jesus washed his disciples' feet, stooping to serve, he has called us to follow his example.

Three Yale University professors lead a highly-sought-after course entitled Life Worth Living, and their course material was eventually published in book form, *Life Worth Living: A Guide to What Matters Most*. They reflect on Jesus' teaching in Luke 6:46–49, that a person who comes to Jesus, hears his words, and acts on them is like a person who laid the foundation of a house on rock, leading to a well-built house, saying, "Hear the words, sure. But the firm foundation isn't the hearing. It's the doing. It's our practices, not just our abstract insights, that we can count on and build on."[3] In drawing conclusions at the book's end, they share this potent truth: "Community is precisely about cultivating ways of life that match practices with values."[4]

Jesus calls us to value compassionately serving others' needs. But more than that, Jesus calls us to live out this value by our practices. How will we react when face-to-face with the needs of others? And will we open ourselves to our BIC community's role (locally, regionally, nationally, and globally) in provoking us to love and good deeds (Hebrews 10:24) so that the practices of our individual and corporate lives may more closely match this value of *Serving Compassionately*?

MOVED WITH COMPASSION

"Words are always fascinating things," according to William Barclay in *New Testament Words*.[5] In the book's preface, Barclay continues,

Translation from one language into another is in one sense impossible. It is always possible to translate words with accuracy when they refer to *things*. A chair is a chair in any language. But it is a different matter when it is a question of *ideas*. In that case, some words need, not another to translate them, but a phrase, or a sentence, or even a paragraph. Further, words have associations. They have associations with people, with history, with ideas, and with other words, and these associations give words a certain flavour which cannot be rendered in translation, but which affects their meaning and significance in the most important way.[6]

Michael Card, in the preface to *Inexpressible: Hesed and the Mystery of God's Lovingkindness*, highlights the complexity of language and translation. Echoing Barclay's thoughts on the associations that enhance our understanding of the meaning of words, Card writes that there are some "words that require paragraphs and parables to provide even a hint of all that they might possibly mean."[7]

One of the Greek words Barclay explains, and one of the words that is helped by "paragraphs and parables" to explore its meaning, is *splagchnizesthai*, which means *to be moved with compassion*. It derives from the noun *splagchna*, which refers to the viscera, the soft internal organs of the body—the heart, the lungs, the liver, and the intestines. The Greeks considered these inner parts, often translated *bowels*, to be the seat of the deepest emotions. This word does not describe ordinary pity or compassion, but an emotion which moves a person to the very depths of their being.[8]

Splagchnizesthai, the strongest word used in the New Testament to represent compassion, is attributed solely to Jesus, with the exception of its use by Jesus three times: the master who had compassion on the servant who was not able to pay his debt; the compassion with which the father welcomed home and embraced his lost son; and the compassion which caused the Samaritan to help the wounded traveler on the road between Jerusalem and Jericho.

The gospel writers primarily used the word *splagchnizesthai* to describe the compassion exhibited by Jesus toward those in need. Jesus was moved with compassion when he saw the harassed and helpless crowds and considered them to be like a sheep without a shepherd and when he saw the needs that the crowds experienced as they followed him out to the desert. Jesus was moved with compassion by the leper who knelt, asking him to make him clean, and by the two blind men sitting by the roadside, begging him to have mercy on them. Jesus was moved with compassion for the widow at Nain who was burying her only son and for the man who appealed to Jesus to heal his epileptic son.

While many other emotions and actions of Jesus were recorded by the gospel writers, their use of this word *splagchnizesthai* in these nine passages shows the kinds of things which deeply moved the heart of Jesus.[9] Jesus had a visceral response to the spiritual lostness of the crowd, to hunger, to physical needs, to pain, and to people's sorrow. Eusebius, in the third century, wrote of Jesus, "He was like some excellent physician, who, in order to cure the sick, examines what is repulsive, handles sores, and reaps pain himself from the sufferings of others."[10] Touched in the deepest part of himself by human need, Jesus exemplified the Latin root word for compassion, *compati*, "suffer with." According to Barclay, Jesus "regarded the sufferer and the needy with a pity which issued in help."[11]

In the ancient Greek world, people would have understood that God, because he was God, could have no feeling. In contrast to this way of thinking, the gospel writers stress the compassion of the Lord Jesus, that God voluntarily chose to feel for and with humankind. Barclay reminds us, "We think it is commonplace that God is love, and that the Christian life is love. We would do well to remember that we would never have known that without the revelation of Jesus Christ, of whom it is so often and so amazingly said that he was moved with compassion."[12]

CLOTHED WITH COMPASSION

The call upon Christians to care about and address the needs of others is found throughout the New Testament. Paul, for instance, instructs the Colossians that when a person becomes a Christian, there ought to be a complete change in them, with a putting off of the old self and a putting on of a new self.

After sharing traits of the old self that are to be done away with, Paul goes on to share that those in Christ are God's chosen ones, holy and beloved (Colossians 3:12). The love and the grace of God have been demonstrated to the whole world through Jesus, extended to the ends of the earth rather than to one chosen nation. As recipients of God's love and grace, as God's chosen, holy, and beloved people, we are to put on the virtues of Christ himself.

The first virtue we are instructed to put on is compassion, the same compassion which moved Jesus to the depths of his being when confronted with people's needs. We are called to relate to others and their needs in the same way that Jesus did. Just as Jesus was grieved by the pain and suffering of people, just as he reached out with compassionate love, touching people no one else would touch, weeping over people's lostness, healing people, feeding people, sharing people's grief, so we are called to do the same as his followers.

In calling us to be clothed with compassion, Paul builds on the ancient concept of covenant, people coming together in solemn agreement. Covenants were legally binding, without exit clauses, signed in blood as a promise to demonstrate unfailing love to one another. People in the Old Testament called this love *hesed,* while New Testament believers knew it as *agapē.*

In addition to signing in blood, the covenant representatives would also exchange outer garments as a symbol of the relationship. In such covenant cultures, clothing represented who you are and what you do, so to exchange clothing was figuratively saying "My identity is now wrapped in you and your identity is now wrapped in me." By urging us to clothe ourselves with compassion, Paul is essentially asking us to put on Jesus' robe of righteousness and to fully identify with Jesus, loving the way Jesus loved.

COMPASSION ENGENDERS ACTION

What should be our compassionate response to needs? In 1 John, the writer makes abundantly clear that our compassion is not just an inner response in the depth of our beings, but it is worked out in what we do. "We know love by this, that he laid down his life for us—and we ought to lay down our lives for the brothers and sisters. How does God's love abide in anyone who has the world's goods and sees a brother or sister in need and yet refuses help? Little children, let us love not in word or speech but in deed and truth" (1 John 3:16–18 NRSVue).

Philip Yancey, in *A Companion in Crisis,* wrote,

"Simply follow Jesus through the gospels and watch his response to a person afflicted with leprosy, a blind beggar by the road, or even a Roman officer whose servant has fallen ill. Always, without exception, he responds with comfort and healing. . . . If we want to know how God feels about people who are suffering. . . all we need do is look at Jesus' compassionate response. God is on their side."[13]

Yancey continues with these compelling words, "Compassion should ultimately lead to action."[14]

Action in the early church

From the beginning of the Christian church, Jesus' followers have responded compassionately to needs. Immediately after Pentecost, new believers held possessions in common, even selling property to meet the needs of others in the community. This legacy of compassionate giving is also reflected in Paul's message to the Ephesians in Acts 20, while he was traveling throughout Macedonia and Achaia to collect gifts from churches for the hurting Jerusalem church. He reminded them that we must support the weak, and shared Jesus' words, "It is more blessed to give than to receive" (Acts 20:35). Paul also commended the Macedonian church in 2 Corinthians 8 for giving even in poverty.

In the second century in Athens, Aristides wrote a letter to the emperor to assuage his worries that these foreigners and followers of a strange religion might cause trouble. Aristides described in great detail what the Christians were like:

They do not keep for themselves the goods entrusted to them. They do not covet what belongs to others. They show love to their neighbours. They do not do to another what they would not wish to have done to themselves. They speak gently to those who oppress them, and in this way they make them their friends. It has become their passion to do good to their enemies. They live in the awareness of their smallness. Every one of them who has anything gives ungrudgingly to the one who has nothing. If they see a travelling stranger, they bring him under their roof. They rejoice over him as over a real brother, for they do not call one another brothers after the flesh, but they know they are brothers in the Spirit and in God. If they hear that one of them is imprisoned or oppressed for the sake of Christ, they take care of all his needs. If possible they set him free. If anyone among them is poor or comes into want while they themselves have nothing to spare, they fast two or three days for him. In this way they can supply any poor man with the food he needs. This, O Emperor, is the rule of life of the Christians, and this is their manner of life.[15]

In the next centuries, Christianity spread in part because of the way Jesus' followers responded to the needs of poor and sick people, which was notably different from the response of those around them. In the latter part of the fourth century, for example, Basil, the bishop of Caesarea, was raising funds to build a place to care for and to love the poor, including isolated and suffering lepers who had lost their relatives, their social status, their livelihoods, their homes, their clothing, and even necessities like food and water. They were considered to be "put together from the same clay. . . made in the image of God,"[16] and thus worthy of being helped.

From the early centuries of the church onward, hostels for travelers and hospices for the sick and the poor were established. By the fifth century, hospitals quickly expanded, with bishops of regions taking the initiative in founding them just as Basil had done.[17] These Christians understood the call to put on the compassion of Christ and to serve the needs of people around them, faithfully living out the words of Jesus.

Action in BIC history

Likewise, the BIC church, during the last 250 years, has lived out the compassion of Jesus in countless ways. BIC home mission work, for instance, which first began in the mid-1890s in urban areas of North America, like Chicago, Philadelphia, Buffalo, San Francisco, Dayton, Des Moines, and Toronto, demonstrated the compassion of Christ through meeting the unique physical and spiritual needs that were part of city living.[18] Jesus' gospel was proclaimed amidst this compassionate service. Devin Manzullo-Thomas, writing about Sarah Bert, who answered the call to serve, shares:

> The bustling metropolis of Chicago—choked by unemployment, flooded with immigrants, and plagued by tenement housing, unjust working conditions, and dangerous vices—was not an easy place to live in the late 19th century. Yet it was the city to which Sarah H. Bert. . . moved in 1894, following God's call. Born in 1860, Bert was a frail, timid Kansas farmgirl who felt the Spirit drawing her to work with the poor and outcast. Against all odds, she made the Windy City her home, ministering there for more than 50 years. . . . Her legacy can be summarized in the words she herself used to describe urban ministry in 1904: "Few would ever get to God if there were no deeds of kindness scattered along their path by Christian hearts and loving hands."[19]

In an 1895 *Evangelical Visitor* article, Bert reported, "In going from place to place we find many poor, destitute, almost starving families. . . with no comforts of life to cheer them, as we have, and not enough clothing to keep them warm, hardly enough fuel to keep from freezing, and lack of daily food. . . . When we see and hear these sad stories it melts our heart in sympathy,"[20] a visceral response mirroring Jesus' response to need.

Shortly after, the church had expanded its mission work beyond the United States. Since that time, BIC churches that were established in Africa, Asia, and other places throughout the world have lived out what the early church had put into practice, that wherever there are worshiping communities, there would also be places to care for the sick and the poor with the compassion of Jesus.

In Zimbabwe and Zambia, for instance, there are medical facilities and schools; medical care is extended and children are educated, bringing improvement to people's lives in two significant areas of need. In India and Nepal, the BIC has directed attention to compassion ministries, providing for the care and education of children. As one example of ministry efforts in Central and South America, the compassionate work of the BIC church in Nicaragua has included a health clinic, adult literacy, and community development projects.[21] And on the streets of Madrid, the church in recent years has reached out to feed hungry people and to pray, bringing the healing power of Christ to people with physical, emotional, and relational ailments. In all of the places throughout the world where we have planted churches, the compassion of Jesus has inspired and motivated the development of ministries.

THE CHALLENGING CHOICE TO SERVE COMPASSIONATELY

In every place, in every age, serving the needs of others with compassion has been a choice that followers of Christ have been called to make, a choice illustrated perhaps most profoundly by the story which Jesus shared in Luke 10 of the man who was attacked as he traveled from Jerusalem to Jericho and was in need of care. In contrast to the priest and the Levite who went on their own way, the Samaritan man, living out what Martin Luther King Jr. has referred to as "dangerous unselfishness,"[22] had mercy on the injured man, and Jesus' instruction at the end of his storytelling was succinct, "Go and do likewise," (Luke 10:37). We do, however, experience challenges in our choice to serve.

The challenge of overindulgence

We face many challenges to choosing compassion. Perhaps most prevalent is the ever-present temptation of overindulgence. This is not a new challenge—Ezekiel's words reveal the persistence of this issue through all generations: "Now this was the sin of your sister Sodom: She and her daughters were arrogant, overfed and unconcerned; they did not help the poor and needy" (Ezekiel 16:49 NIV).

The statistics of our overindulgence in the United States are staggering. "We are bombarded every day by marketing messages urging us to buy, buy, buy. And we do. Way, way too much for most of us."[23] As individuals, families, and congregations simplify our lifestyles, we free up resources previously used on ourselves, allowing us the freedom to contribute toward needs we encounter.

Author Christine Platt shares that homes, décor, productivity, wardrobes, and even digital spaces give opportunity to practice minimalism, and the desired result is "minimizing excess to ensure life is filled with only what matters."[24] While "only what matters" in her book refers to "things we need, use, and love," in our thinking it could simultaneously refer to intangibles, like compassion, generosity, and love—things that truly matter. Platt further shares, "Considering a life with less when we've been constantly encouraged to acquire more requires a serious shift in perspective, priorities, and purpose."[25] Our core value of *Serving Compassionately* is the catalyst for just that kind of needed shift in our thinking, our values, and our behavior.

The challenge of oversaving

North American culture also strongly emphasizes the need to save, for retirement years, education costs of children, emergencies, larger purchases, home down payments, and tomorrow's unknown needs. Saving is encouraged by God, who says, "Precious treasure remains in the house of the wise, but the fool devours it" (Proverbs 21:20). But the wisdom of saving instead of devouring all of the resources at our disposal must be tempered by compassion for the needs of others.

We ought not to be living so future-oriented that we miss opportunities to share our resources to meet needs before us. The young boy who offered his loaves and fish to Jesus might have considered his family's need for food for the next day and kept them to himself, but instead he shared. We are reminded in 1 Timothy, "They are to do good, to be rich in good works, generous, and ready to share, thus storing up for themselves the treasure of a good foundation for the future, so that they may take hold of the life that really is life" (1 Timothy 6:18–19).

Some of our oversaved resources could provide the answers to the needs and prayers of hungry children, sick and dying people who have no access to medical care, those without safe water, those without shelter or warmth, those without school fees. Strengthening our cash position—whether individually, congregationally, or denominationally—must be kept in balance by the priorities of carrying one another's burdens and ministering wholistically in a complex and needy world.

Compelling are the words of Jesus, who put it this way: "Do not store up for yourselves treasures on earth, where moth and rust consume and where thieves break in and steal" (Matthew 6:19). Basil of Caesarea, put it this way in the fourth century:

> That bread which you keep belongs to the hungry; that coat which you preserve in your wardrobe, to the naked; those shoes which are rotting in your possession, to the shoeless; that gold which you have hidden in the ground, to the needy. Wherefore as often as you are able to help others, and refuse, so often did you do them wrong.[26]

And Grace Holland, in describing her BIC upbringing, shared that her mother, who was the daughter of mission workers in Dayton, taught, "It doesn't do any good to save so much if we don't give it away!"[27]

The challenge of superiority

In Luke's portrayal of the Last Supper, the disciples dispute about who among them is the greatest. After years of being with Jesus, witnessing his selflessness and love, the disciples still miss the mark here—vying for position in the kingdom, comparing themselves against one another.

We are not unlike those first disciples, facing the temptation to assert our superiority over others. Thinking of those being served as "lowly" is something we must consciously resist. Since we are not better than those we may be serving, we must throw away any competitive thoughts, making the conscious choice to dignify others. Susan Holman, author of *God Knows There's Need: Christian Responses to Poverty*, urges us to practice true empathy, which she calls a *lateral experience* that is "incompatible with the condescension or 'looking down on' others that often characterizes pity."[28]

The gospel breaks down barriers that humanity erects, reorienting us toward oneness. Howard Thurman, in *Jesus and the Disinherited*, observes "that whenever a need is laid bare, those who stand in the presence of it can be confronted with the experience of universality that makes all class and race distinctions impertinent."[29] All people in all places need food, water, clothing, shelter, education, medical care, safety, and the like. And none of us is exempt from the possibility of trauma, tragedy, and loss. The givers of compassion today may face circumstances which would cause them to be the recipients of compassion tomorrow. There should be no superiority in serving, only love for one another.

The challenge of callousness

We live in a world that is more connected than ever, making it easy to see the impact of natural disasters; war; climate change; oppression based on race, ethnicity, or gender; and abuse in its many forms. We can get so used to hearing about and seeing tragedy that we become numb or hardened toward need.

In contrast, do we, like Jesus, have a visceral response to the resulting needs before us? Are we moved with compassion to sit with, suffer alongside, and be safe places for people? We must resist our hearts growing callous because of our exposure to the many needs in our communities and our world. Jesus can keep us sensitive to the plight of others as he removes from us "the heart of stone" and gives us a heart of flesh (Ezekiel 36:26).

The challenge of feeling overwhelmed

Because our world is more connected than ever, the overabundance of news can paralyze us. Hearing of suffering near and far, we can become overwhelmed, not unlike the disciples in

Mark 6 who were overwhelmed at the prospect of feeding the thousands who were hungry. We want to help, but often do not know how, or we feel as if what we do will not make a big enough difference. An African proverb offers perspective, saying, *How do you eat an elephant? One bite at a time.* The *Serving Compassionately* value compels us to pray, then take the bite we can.

The challenge of people's differences

Differences among people—from language, culture, race, religion, age, politics, economics, education, and employment, to more earthy differences like hygiene, odors, foods, ability and disability, health, sobriety, neighborhoods, and the like—can potentially cause ideological, emotional, and physical distance between people. Such distance engenders fear, misunderstanding, and stereotyping and causes us to want to insulate and keep ourselves safe from discomfort. But that is not Jesus' way. Confronted by needs of those whose situation might naturally repel us, we have been sent into the world as ambassadors for Christ (2 Corinthians 5:20), and Christ's love compels us (2 Corinthians 5:14).

Jesus' treatment of lepers, the ultimate outcast, inspires our service. Max Lucado reimagines the opening chapter of Mark's story of the leper healed by Jesus, from the leper's view:

> Before he spoke, I knew he cared. Somehow I knew he hated this disease as much as, no—more—than I hate it. My rage became trust, and my anger became hope.
>
> From behind a rock, I watched him descend a hill. Throngs of people followed him. I waited until he was only paces from me, then I stepped out.
>
> "Master!"

He stopped and looked in my direction as did dozens of others. A flood of fear swept across the crowd. Arms flew in front of faces. Children ducked behind parents. "Unclean!" someone shouted. . . . But I scarcely heard them. I scarcely saw them. Their panic I'd seen a thousand times. His compassion, however, I'd never beheld. Everyone stepped back except him. He stepped toward me. *Toward* me.[30]

A BETTER CHALLENGE

The example and inspiration of the BIC church through generations provide for us a better challenge, one we should continue to embrace today.

In 1944, at the time of the Chicago Mission's fiftieth anniversary, Joel Carlson, whose young life had been impacted by the ministry of that work, wrote in the *Evangelical Visitor*: "As the youngest member of the Carlson family, we were conscious of the debt of gratitude our family had, for the kindly interest of the Mission, especially during earlier days, when our home was broken by death, first of my father, and then of my mother." Carlson, who was then serving in pastoral ministry at Messiah Lighthouse Chapel in Harrisburg, further shared, "We now know that [city mission work] is not easy work; nevertheless, we still believe that it is work which ought to be done."[31]

At the two hundredth anniversary of the BIC church, church leaders described the heritage of service that had been lived out in those two centuries and called us to continued compassionate service following the example of Jesus. Martin Schrag's General Conference sermon stated our calling succinctly: "Jesus became a *servant* engaging in a healing, teaching, preaching, sharing and forgiving ministry. So must

His flock."[32] And Emerson Lesher, representing the younger generation of leaders, shared:

> Another challenge is for us to be a servant church to the needy people of the world. It will continue to be difficult for us, being largely a white middle-class church, to minister and serve the spiritually, economically, psychologically, and socially poor as Christ did. While the Brethren in Christ may be most effective in witnessing to the white middle class, that is no reason to avoid a ministry to urban and third world people.[33]

Today, almost fifty years since that time, brothers and sisters continue to work and to give in order to meet these challenges in the United States and around the world. There are countless glimpses of the compassion of Christ touching and transforming lives through the preaching of God's Word, providing medical care for the sick, caring for the orphaned, feeding the hungry, ministering to those in prison, housing the homeless, providing relief, teaching children, befriending the lonely, and breaking down barriers that have divided people. While we rejoice in the work that has been done, as well as in the more diverse body the BIC is becoming, the challenge issued continues, and we must continue to labor, give, and serve with the compassion of Christ.

A CHANCE TO HELP

Lewis and Gladys Sider, missionaries sent from the United States to Zimbabwe, met a young girl in 1954 during Lewis's visit to village schools. According to his daughter, Harriet Bicksler,

> [Lewis] describes noticing a girl sitting in the front row who had difficulty seeing the blackboard. . . . "Somehow, I

developed a feeling that she needed special help and also I had the conviction that she had real ability."[34]

This girl, Makanalia Dhlamini:

was eventually able to get glasses for her poor eyesight, earn enough money from working to pay her school fees, attend school, and receive a teaching certificate. [Lewis] describes her accomplishments: "She has been a teacher for many years. . . a teacher of special education for the handicapped in Bulawayo. . . . She has helped to start both the Lobengula and the Bulawayo Central churches in Bulawayo. She has been a wonderful wife, mother, teacher, and example of Christian character and leadership."[35]

Makanalia was part of the contingent of BICC Zimbabwe who traveled to the United States to attend Mennonite World Conference in 2015. While in Pennsylvania, Makanalia spent time with the Siders' daughter, requesting that Harriet take her to the gravesite of her parents; it had been her prayer to see where Lewis and Gladys had lived and where they are buried. Makanalia knelt at the burial site of the missionaries who had such a profound impact on her life for the glory of Christ and prayed; the words of her prayer capture the essence of our core value of *Serving Compassionately*: "Let me pass the Word to all I come across. Help me, Lord, to love those who are estranged. Let me love the poor, let me love the fatherless, the orphans, those who have nothing. I didn't have anything when Lewis Sider picked me up. I had nothing. There are many in Africa with nothing, who have no school fees. I've had a chance. Give me a chance to help them like Lewis."[36]

May Makanalia's words also be the prayer of each of our hearts, "Give me a chance to help."

· · · · · · · · · · · · · · · · ·

RESPONSE ESSAY

Serving Compassionately

▶ *Thobekile Ncube, Bulawayo, Zimbabwe*

In my context, *Serving Compassionately* means to recognize the needs of other people and to help. In helping, Brethren in Christ Zimbabwe seeks to address immediate needs in our villages and cities as well as develop long-term skills and knowledge among people to help alleviate future need.

SERVING PHYSICAL NEEDS

One of the greatest physical needs is access to food. Feeding the hungry is also an opportunity to teach new skills regarding food cultivation. Agricultural sustainability projects help people learn to grow their own food while they also learn to care for the environment. Those in our communities who are physically fit and able to work receive both food and education as an act of love.

Being compassionate is an expected cultural norm, to the extent that when there is sickness in a family, the community visits the home, bringing material necessities such as toiletries, food, or anything that the family might need to help the sick. We believe that everyone has something to offer to those in need. Often, we do not have enough resources, but in our poverty, there is always something that God has blessed us with to minister, be it our service, time, or farm produce.

When there is a funeral, the community contributes in many ways. If it is in a rural area where there is no electricity, neighbors fetch water and firewood in order to cook for the family. This is no small duty; lacking firewood and water means no meals. Hence the sick, elderly and bereaved appreciate when they are helped in this difficult task. We then eat together as we mourn, sing, pray, and read the Bible together for comfort and hope. We also take turns keeping the family company, showing our love and support by being there. If the bereaved need to talk to someone, we give them an ear. All this is done without expecting any rewards. It is an act of feeling empathy for another's grief, just as Jesus felt compassion for the widow burying her son in Luke 7:13.

SERVING SPIRITUAL NEEDS

Voluntary evangelists serve spreading the good news of Jesus. These evangelists preach the Word in shopping malls, on buses, through door-to-door evangelism, and street-preaching. They are driven by love and passion to serve, offering their time to reach the spiritually lost among us. Much like in the gospel of Matthew, when Jesus responds to the lostness of the crowd, "When he saw the crowds, he had compassion on them, because they were harassed and helpless, like sheep without a shepherd" (Matthew 9:36 NIV).

The Ubuntu proverb, *I am what I am because of who we all are* culturally expresses the value of *Serving Compassionately* in our churches. Serving is a whole community effort intended to reach everyone. Foremost, relationships bond us as a community. More important than being individualistic, we must care for one another. No one should be found naked in a community where Ubuntu is embraced! It is a disgrace. We should be found covering each other's nakedness without announcing it publicly, for the sake of the community.

PRACTICING COMPASSION

I grew up in a rural area at the Mampara line near Mtshabezi Mission, a BIC Mission Station. I was raised up by my maternal grandmother, a very compassionate, hospitable woman. She was well-known in the community for her kindness and generosity. Her home attracted strangers and those who knew her, to the extent that we always had visitors with us. My brother and I worked alongside Grandma preparing meals, washing dishes, cleaning, and heating warm bath water for our visitors. Grandma helped anyone who came to our home, including Christians, non-Christians, strangers, and extended family members.

Surprisingly, during these frequent visits, we never ran out of food, even if we thought we would. She always taught us, "Isihambi kasiqedi kudla," translated, "A visitor does not finish food." And, "Isisu somhambi kasinganani, singango phonjwana lwembuzi," meaning, "A traveler's stomach is not that big, it is the size of the hollow in a goat's horn." The hollow in a goat's horn is very small and fills quickly. In other words, the expression meant that a traveler will not empty your house of food, hence they deserve to be fed anytime.

Grandma intended for these sayings to be instructive, showing us the value of *Serving Compassionately*. In her serving, Grandma did not surrender to the fear that the food source would run out. She was not limited by the fear of scarcity; in fact, she would often pack extra food for visitors to take and share with their families.

I am reminded of Jesus feeding the five thousand in Matthew 14:13–21. Jesus' compassion, which came from within, provided for and fed the crowd. Admittedly, there are some people in Zimbabwe who sometimes behave carelessly, like the disciples did in this story.

Severe economic crisis affected Zimbabwe in 2008 and the country has not recovered, experiencing intermittent periods of hyperinflation and high levels of unemployment. These economic realities are all-consuming and impact our ability to see and meet the needs around us in a compassionate way. Some people are embracing selfish modes of giving, and no longer seem to have a heart for the needy. They feel a strong need to protect what they have, even though they know the truth and have been taught well the compassion of Jesus. The Zimbabwean people can learn a good lesson here; Jesus provided for a large crowd from five small loaves of bread and two small fish! Our poverty and prolonged economic crisis cannot be an excuse for not serving compassionately. When we think this way, we are limiting God, for his word says, "It is more blessed to give than to receive" (Acts 20:35b).

. . . .
RESPONSE ESSAY

Serving Compassionately

▶ *Drew and Millyellen Strayer, Salem, Oregon*

As we reflect on this value, we are of the same spirit as the authors, affirming the path of stepping stones from God's compassion, Christ's teaching and example, the teaching and example of the early church, the messages by ecumenical writers today, as well as the unique voice the BIC lends to the value *Serving Compassionately*.

In our practice of compassionate service, we lean on the teachings and actions of Jesus, who was "moved with compassion" to lovingly serve those around him. Within the parables, Jesus encourages us to give without expecting repayment. We viscerally experience this *splagchnizesthai* in the depths of our being, within our home, church, community, and world.

Early in the essay, the authors' question challenges us to evaluate, "Will we open ourselves to our BIC community's role. . . so that the practices of our individual and corporate lives may more closely match this value, *Serving Compassionately*?" Throughout BIC history we see examples of compassionate service in the United States and around the world. Some traveled to their location of service while others were called to remain in their place. Once settled, they cared for their neighbors in need of sustenance and support, while also attending to their need of hope, truth, and life-change that Christ makes possible. Driven and compelled by the compassion of Christ and encouraged by the example of our BIC predecessors who clothed themselves with compassion (Colossians 3:12), we moved across the country back to a city we knew, to church plant a neighborhood expression of Christ's love in Salem, Oregon.

COMPASSION IN THE NEIGHBORHOOD

As disciples of Jesus Christ, the Holy Spirit resides within us and blesses us with gifts to compassionately serve in gentleness, patience, peace, and joy, allowing ourselves to be interrupted by God and interrupted by people made in his image. In our neighborhood, we see people in the grips of witchcraft, elemental spirit worship, eastern religion worship, distrust of neighbors, judgmentalism, generational poverty, and houselessness. In this place, we seek to be an expression of Christ's compassion by inviting all neighbors to come together for our front-yard barbecues to build community, break down walls of isolation, build trust, and tell of the freedom in Christ Jesus. The Holy Spirit reminds us that our identity is wrapped up in Jesus, not in our own comforts. Time after time, compassion prompts action even when we are exhausted or inconvenienced.

Within our context, we answer when the doorbell rings to provide food to neighbors even when we have just sat down as a family to eat. We hold hands to pray with a person battling addiction and houselessness who would like her family to be blessed and to personally feel worth. We recharge neighbors' car batteries, are loving foster parents, and fix the tire of a teenager's bike or skateboard countless times. We pray a blessing over a neighbor who has a political or spiritual agenda that opposes the light of Jesus Christ, and turn a conversation from gossip or ill will to focus instead on kind views of others. These are the neighbors we invite into our home for conversation to explore Jesus together. We are commanded to love our enemy and pray for those who persecute us (Matthew 5:44), bless those who curse us, and pray for those who mistreat us (Luke 6:28).

When one of us is serving a neighbor, the other is praying for discernment and strength for the one ministering, because it can take a toll. But we rejoice in the opportunity and choose to be interruptible. We choose to sacrifice, to love in difficult situations in our home and in our neighborhood. "Let us not become weary in doing good, for at the proper time we will reap a harvest if we do not give up. Therefore, as we have opportunity, let us do good to all people, especially to those who belong to the family of believers" (Galatians 6:9–10 NIV). Clearly, those in Galatia were weary, and so Paul encouraged them.

Compassion prompts us to step out of our home to be in contact with those around us. This hot summer as we walked to the park to offer popsicles to houseless neighbors there, one older man smiled and exclaimed, "I haven't had a popsicle since I was a kid." Another houseless neighbor replied, "See, I told you they were nice Christians." We, the church, desire to be known as disciples of Jesus by our love (John 13:35), not hate, exclusion, or divisiveness.

SERVING AMID THE CHALLENGES

We acknowledge the challenges to compassionate service described by the authors as they identify both the individualistic focus of American culture as well as the contemporary religious norms that prioritize personal and family safety above sharing the gospel. We testify to the challenges of callousness and feeling overwhelmed because of constant digital access to all the world's joys but also its sufferings. This can bring about apathy, weariness or fatigue. But we remind ourselves to keep our eyes on Jesus the author and perfecter of our faith (Hebrews 12:2). None of us are superior to one another whether in the body of Christ, within our denomination, nor among anyone we serve compassionately. God has planted each one of us in our contexts to love in the ways our neighbors need, whoever our neighbors may be.

Part of the compassionate servanthood of Christ came because he was interruptible. He was moved with compassion despite being amid other commitments. Christ healed and ministered to those who interrupted his walking and teaching all the time. Christ knew and modeled the essential truth that we must follow—be ready always to love and serve with compassion.

. . . .
CHAPTER 7

Discussion Questions

1. Define compassion; describe one way you have experienced compassion; and describe one way you have demonstrated compassion.

2. Why do you think it is important to model Jesus-like compassion when we serve?

3. If your worship community, family, and you were all removed from your town/city and neighborhood, would your neighbors notice? Would you be missed? Why or why not?

4. In the essay, self-indulgence, oversaving, superiority, callousness, the discomfort of people's differences, and feeling overwhelmed are all named as possible hindrances to more compassionate living. Which of these remains a stumbling block for you and what are ways you can remove your hindrance?

5. Name one person who has left a compassionate legacy. Share the lessons you have learned from that person; describe the legacy you would like to leave.

CHAPTER 8

Pursuing Peace

José Otamendi

We value all human life and promote forgiveness, under-
standing, reconciliation, and nonviolent resolution of conflict.

INTRODUCTION: NOSTALGIA FOR EDEN

Beginning the hardest period of the COVID-19 pandemic, I
traveled to the nearby coast to visit my brother-in-law and his
wife. It was exciting to see the sea again, even though it was
misty. Although the scene did not make the intense impression
on me as when I was a child, coming down from the mountains
and out of the highway tunnels, that incredibly blue, mysteri-
ous, overwhelming, and beautiful stripe lifted me again to that
sublime feeling of ineffable beauty and happiness. A longing
for something beyond the tumultuous experience of everyday
life. It was the emotion of someone who recovers the reality of
a happy and beautiful memory.

The immensity, the power, the beauty and fullness of life is
still there. It is real, it is not a dream. As in a kaleidoscope, several images, emotions, and sense of wonder reflect the beauty
and the longing for an authentic and permanent bliss.

In Revelation chapter 21 it is said that, at the end of this
age, the sea will no longer exist. I am very sorry that John the

Apocalyptic was so afraid of the sea that he could announce the Creator would eliminate it. But there is also a great emotion in that spectacle of majestic beauty that the prophet describes in his vision of the world, created anew so that humanity lives in eternal peace and perfect health with its Creator:

> Then I saw a new heaven and a new earth; for the first heaven and the first earth had passed away, and the sea was no more. And I saw the holy city, the new Jerusalem, coming down out of heaven from God, prepared as a bride adorned for her husband. And I heard a loud voice from the throne saying,
>
> "See, the home of God is among mortals.
> He will dwell with them;
> they will be his peoples,
> and God himself will be with them;
> he will wipe every tear from their eyes.
> Death will be no more;
> mourning and crying and pain will be no more,
> for the first things have passed away."
> (Revelation 21:1–4)

The apocalyptic John had a vision of greater grandeur than the violent revelations of heaven and earth could offer. We all have this incredible longing for peace, the *shalom* from God, the absolute bliss. It is like we always want to return to Eden. Yes, we all have nostalgia for Eden. The earthly paradise, regardless of whether one believes in its geographical existence or not, is rather a state of existence that we all yearn for. We long for full confidence in a nonthreatening environment, where there will be no violence against us, nor will we make war against others.

But reality is discouraging: wars, thefts, abuses, negligence, and the duplicitous desire to hurt. Violence can also be verbal,

with soft words, but loaded with ill will or a smiling wicked-
ness and "kind" abuse of power. The gates of Eden appear to
remain closed to us as if we were migrants from disaster who
cannot enter the Promised Land.

Yet, through this yearning for peace and security we cling
to the words of Jesus on the cross, when he promised the thief,
"Truly I tell you, today you will be with me in Paradise" (Luke
23:43). It seems that we understand only the eschatological (or
future) aspect of that promise, leaving aside the present truth
affirmed in Scripture that God is our peace. That peace of Eden
is God's *shalom*, the Creator's gift to us, our complete, integral
existence in communion with him. That is why we should not
understand *shalom* only as peace. Shalom is not just peace, but
perfection, completeness. It means being in good relationship
with God, but also with people, with the environment. More-
over, the environment will then overflow with the blessing of
the Creator. There is health, fertility, well-being, security. "Let
me hear what God the LORD will speak, for he will speak
peace to his people, to his faithful, to those who turn to him in
their hearts" (Psalm 85:8).

Shalom, the divine gift of peace, then, is an intimate state
and a social situation that we can experience in the here and
now where the contradictions between our attitudes, emotions
and thoughts have dissolved, becoming coherent with God's
will, in such a way that we cannot desire violence and revenge.

WATCHING FROM THE AGES

Although war is not the only expression of violence, it is the
most destructive of all its forms. It inspires a sense of awe
that comes from the horror of destruction and cruelty at
its most. Reaction to this panorama of annihilation is fear,
anger, distress.

Take, for example, the tragedy of the Great War (World War I), stripped of its romantic and patriotic cover of aggressive nationalism. The dread of the trenches, the infernal trauma of living with the rotting dead, the physical and mental impairment, and the death of young people. The great irony of this tragedy is that it contradicted the religious identity of the nations involved in this war: Western Christian nations. This conflagration showed for the first time the amazing capacity of the human race to extend industrial power massively to cause death and destruction at a new level.

It seemed that such a madness would never happen again. But only twenty-one years later, the devastation of war would swallow even more lives. It causes chills to suppose that another great world war could break out, because this time perhaps there will be no way to rebuild a humanity so miserably destroyed.

Centuries before these modern tragedies, Christianity having become the religion of European countries, Christians engaged in war against those who professed a different faith. The Crusades were the most ironic and absurd movement to represent the alleged love for Christ, for the warriors acted not just as common Christians, but as "soldiers for the cross;" they killed people, sacked villages and cities, and thanked God for their gory victories:

> Raymond [of Aguilers] portrayed this pornographic bloodshed in terms of sacrifice, specifying that "in the Temple our men were wading up to their ankles in enemy blood," that some 320 corpses were set ablaze as a burnt offering, and that the slaughter began on Friday at the ninth hour, when Jesus was crucified.[1]

Why do we engage in war? Perhaps we still believe in the violent "resolution" of conflicts, seeking dominance to silence the opponent? This terrible tradition of destroying the other in order to dominate them is more than a purely material or cultural impulse. It is a tragic spiritual problem caused by the fracture of that most intimate and authentic relationship with God that Jesus revealed to us. That is why Christianity cannot be fully understood nor developed individually unless spiritual conversion makes a profound change in us.

Our attitude of dominance and aggression needs something powerful to make it transcend both its biological limits and the heritage of social and individual dominance. It needs to be pushed beyond that limit so as to make radical change actually take place. This transformation of our inherited violence can only be attained by an intimate supernatural conversion. This implies a process whose relevant expressions we can see in Scripture. In obedience to what God revealed, in order to search out an honest and effective piety, men and women started what we call today the Radical Reformation.

The Anabaptist heritage

Through history, even in our days, we see how retaliation, bloodshed, and taking justice into one's own hand is learned, and is massively oriented towards its social and individual implementation. On the other hand, emotional forces of anger, hate, and revenge become institutional, apparently "civilized." However, they keep a root firmly entrenched in models of retaliation as justice.

How do we break with that? How does the human will, with its "normal" desire for revenge and dominance, break down in favor of a consistent, coherent, determined, and inspired search for reconciliation and peace?

Nearly five hundred years ago, the first Anabaptists radically broke with the use of weapons and force against their fellow brothers and sisters. They were inspired by Jesus and his words in the Sermon on the Mount, and their love for God had made their hearts and minds unwilling to obey the violent traditions of human justice. They differentiated between the kingdom of this world and the kingdom of God, whose spiritual reality they were rediscovering in the Scriptures. Following the teaching of Jesus in Matthew 5:38–39, the Swiss Brethren group that promulgated the Schleitheim Confession affirmed in its fourth article their renouncement of the use of weapons against other men:

> Thereby shall also fall away from us the diabolical weapons of violence—such as sword, armor, and the like, and all of their use to protect friends or against enemies—by virtue of the word of Christ: "you shall not resist evil."[2]

As they decided to break the cycle of violence by radically applying the teachings of Jesus in the Sermon on the Mount, they broke the cycle of using violence as a means to do justice. Although this attracted the anger of others and made them perfect scapegoats, their amazing decision to faithfully follow Jesus and his teaching on peace started a spiritual movement for peace and the respect that resulted in a more authentic Christian life.

The maintenance of this essential principle of nonresistance has kept at bay institutional and personal violence from those who follow this categorical conviction for peace. The somber aspect in this is always the fact that, being unarmed, rejecting the use of force against others, they could easily become the victims that would never oppose their enemies. But then there is acceptance of suffering by following the example of Jesus himself: "When he was abused, he did not return abuse; when he suffered, he did not threaten; but he entrusted himself to the one who judges justly" (1 Peter 2:23).

And, prophetically, the Anabaptists adopted the under-standing of the suffering servant in Isaiah 53 as the suffering Jesus: "He was oppressed, and he was afflicted, yet he did not open his mouth; like a lamb that is led to the slaughter, and like a sheep that before its shearers is silent, so he did not open his mouth" (Isaiah 53:7).

One of the spiritual roots that we, the BIC, have is Ana-baptism. That is why we value this process of moving from the exercise of violence to the practice of reconciliation and nonresistance.

It occurs in two conjugated spheres, both personal and insti-tutional: a deep desire to make and maintain peace, increasing the sense of love, compassion and solidarity with others. That is personal and human. And then the supernatural strength and discernment, which compels us to a life of holiness that can only be explained through the allegories and metaphors that Scripture presents to us as divine revelation: "So if anyone is in Christ, there is a new creation: everything old has passed away; see, everything has become new!" (2 Corinthians 5:17).

EMBRACING PEACE

Peaceful does not mean *pacifist*; and *pacifist* does not mean *Christian* either. Yet both terms are intimately related to Chris-tian life as the principle that we are not to be aggressive in our relationships. This attitude is more a posture of the heart than hard self-taught discipline, meaning that necessarily the grace of God should have transformed us inwardly before we experience the surrender of our emotional, spiritual, and physical weapons, with which we inflict pain on others. And that includes not only institutional, religious, or social peace, but also the necessary peace in our daily walk as family and coworkers. Notice the order and sense of Paul's apostolic blessing at the end of 2 Corinthians: "The grace of the Lord Jesus Christ, the love of God, and the communion of the Holy Spirit be with all of you" (2 Corinthians 13:13).

This does not mean that we receive those gifts from God in that exact order; rather it shows how eminent Paul regarded the experiencing of God's grace in our lives. It is divine grace that leads us to receive salvation and peace with God, as expressed in the BIC core value *Experiencing God's Love and Grace*. This is a peace from the soul, a peace that flows from the most intimate part of our being, a peace that comes first from being reconciled to God. In this bliss not only are we freed from hostility against God, but that we are no longer at war with ourselves either:

> Therefore, since we are justified by faith, we have peace with God through our Lord Jesus Christ, through whom we have obtained access to this grace in which we stand; and we boast in our hope of sharing the glory of God (Romans 5:1–2).

Nonetheless, this deep peace occurs only after an authentic and profound conversion of the individual. This also translates into an attitude that Paul exposes in this way in his letter to the Galatians:

> I have been crucified with Christ; and it is no longer I who live, but it is Christ who lives in me. And the life I now live in the flesh I live by faith in the Son of God, who loved me and gave himself for me (Galatians 2:19–20).

This self-acceptance begins with the exclusion of any intimate self-rejection, with accepting oneself under God's grace, with being aware of an unassuming existence, where *unassuming* becomes a spiritual synonym of inner peace: We have been cleansed of the emotional and spiritual turmoil that affected us. However, this unassuming existence is not simple at all. This is one of the spiritual paradoxes of being human. It is about being free internally in order to rid others of our contempt and the aggressive defense of ourselves. "Blessed are the pure in heart, for they will see God" (Matthew 5:8).

This process is supernatural: it is not accomplished by hard work and perseverance, but rather we are propelled, or brought quietly, and sometimes even suddenly, to the edge of ourselves, to the edge of our ego, by a loving, supernatural force that comes from within, the holy presence of the Lord in us. It is like looking at the transformed reality of a world that no longer reflects us but reflects the precious image of our Creator. The prayer that brings us to this state is not one of grandiloquence or arrogance, nor is it one of believing ourselves superior to others. It is the prayer that brings us in a calm and conscious way to the presence of God, our Creator, our Light, our Source of Life.

In the bliss of that divine encounter, we are liberated of any kind of attachment, the mundane models that we unconsciously incorporate by virtue of social traditions. Anger, greed, but also emotional pain should recede day after day, until we notice (and other people will notice as well) that there is a progressive, positive, transformation of ourselves:

> But, as it is written,
> "What no eye has seen, nor ear heard,
> nor the human heart conceived,
> what God has prepared for those who love him"—
> these things God has revealed to us through the Spirit;
> for the Spirit searches everything, even the depths of God
> (1 Corinthians 2:9–10).

Does this mean that we are to drop any social or community efforts to prevent violence in the world? Of course not. Peace organizations, diffusion of peace and reconciliation values through books, workshops, conferences, and videos, all of this is important, and can work as bridgeheads to conquer the terrain of concord. The missions that are carried out as mediation projects for peace, palliatives in case of war, protection against abuse, torture, persecution: all this enormous, real, effective, gigantic effort would multiply exponentially if it were possible, in some way, to spread the message of peace as a real experience, not just a message in the conceptual sense, but a real, experiential message of love for the other.

But although these are important tools and means to create awareness in this regard, an authentic, radical change cannot take place if there is not a true, profound change of the individual. This radically will transform our perception of both creation and Creator, awakening a sense of how sacred people are.

This cannot be understood as a recent humanistic development, something that did not exist at the time and environment of Jesus, but rather as a blossoming of God's revelation to his people through his Spirit, sent by the Father and the Son. An important, integral part of understanding God's revelation to the human being is realizing the Johannine saying, "I am the way, and the truth, and the life. No one comes to the Father except through me" (John 14:6). This is far more than an expression of Jesus' uniqueness; it is the revelation of our need to relate to that incommensurable source of our existence that brings divine Light to our otherwise worldly life.

The gospel of Jesus Christ is irreplaceable. This is not a kind of evangelical chauvinism, but the conviction that, beyond the ties of labels and dogmas developed over the centuries, an internal, individual change becomes evident in our souls, through a miraculous intuition. Like what the prodigal experienced, it is a coming to oneself, realizing how miserably the rags and stink of our pride threatens us every day. We pray in the Lord's Prayer "And lead us not into temptation, but deliver us from evil," and that is quite necessary since spiritual blindness could make of us a spiritual wretch.

In those moments of transformation, a power flourishes that is not ours, but that acts in us, transforming our way of thinking and behaving, leading us to firmly remain faithful to the fundamental core of that gospel. Otherwise, the overwhelming violence of the world and the overwhelming memories of our previous behavior patterns would divert us from the goal, which is to merge our will with the will of God, in sacred communion, hallowed by the Holy Spirit. His living presence illuminates our heart in the most intimate part of us, prompting us to yearn for the image of God that beats in our hearts, constantly calling us to meet him: "And all of us, with unveiled faces, seeing the glory of the Lord as though reflected in a mirror, are being transformed into the same image from one degree of glory to another; for this comes from the Lord, the Spirit" (2 Corinthians 3:18).

FOSTERING DEEP PEACE

Religion is a system in which people, their beliefs, ideas, and practices, are organized according to what is legitimate within that system. If a religion, denomination, or individual congregation only maintains its legitimacy institutionally and does not deepen its worldview through a spiritual praxis that leads to authentic spirituality, then it would only be showing its purely sociocultural face. This would not help its participants to transcend their daily human limitation, since religion without spirituality is just culture. Traditions, no matter how sublime they may seem, cannot be a substitute for authentic spirituality. In order not to let religion stagnate in an institution with a political-religious structure that has lost its soul, it is essential to cultivate the spirituality of its members.

Jesus, though a Torah-observant Jew, was well aware of how religious postures can mask worldly intentions, and he urged his followers to radically change their hostile attitudes: "So when you are offering your gift at the altar, if you remember that your brother or sister has something against you, leave your gift there before the altar and go; first be reconciled to your brother or sister, and then come and offer your gift" (Matthew 5:23–24). Which is a saying that resonates with the word of the prophet Hosea: "For I desire steadfast love and not sacrifice, the knowledge of God rather than burnt-offerings" (Hosea 6:6).

Spirituality is the state of our relationship with God: believing, staying within what is morally and ethically acceptable, preserving our communion with him, and being aware of his presence in our daily life. That would express and nurture our spirituality.

The conviction that led Anabaptists to risk their lives and the lives of their loved ones was not understood as religion, but rather as spirituality. The only way we can maintain the spiritual dimension of seeking peace, and also the reconciliation in troubled times, is by keeping a profound awareness of God's presence in our lives, in our words, in compassion. This is a true apostolate that every Christian must carry out; because there are people in the world who are being hurt, abused, and even enslaved on a daily basis.

And that is what we do when we persevere in our vision of peace and reconciliation as something sacred, a gift from God that must be shared and expanded. The deep peace that comes from Jesus will transform our lives, and our world. This process starts with a working of the Spirit in our hearts, leading us sometimes to situations we never thought of, as we can see in the next true story.

An experience of compassion

For years, Martin had had a difficult relationship with John, who had behaved unfairly towards him, causing him emotional and work damage. Even so, being a Christian, Martin tolerated him, helped him on many occasions and had a half affection for him, in a chiaroscuro that showed signs of resentment. This means that his forgiveness had not reached the point where he felt freed from the sadness and animosity that John inspired with his behavior.

That was the case until the day John lost a loved one, very close to him, in tragic circumstances. True to his intercessory habit, Martin found himself praying for John and his family. But at some point, guided partly by his feelings and partly by something that was pulling him in a new direction, he was overcome with an intense emotion of compassion. He broke into tears, crying while a real sadness overwhelmed him in two different ways: for the pain of his Christian brother, and for having kept in his heart that resentment against him.

This was repentance, pure, inescapable. This was different from the kindheartedness he had felt, and to this day he cannot clearly explain what had moved him to a deeper sense of mercy and empathy for John. John had not changed his attitude, nor had Martin forgotten the past of their relationship; but that experience put everything in a new perspective: an authentic and deep compassion for the one who, even though he was the one who had hurt him, was a creature in need of understanding and love, a love and understanding that was beyond his normal human will. Martin recognized that what he felt now had its origin in the presence of Jesus.

It is necessary, however, to note that it is not about pity, but about compassion: suffering together with those who suffer. An important element in this experience is identifying with the sufferer as an equal who needs and deserves our attention and help. This experience does not lead to a sense of satisfaction or well-being. On the contrary, it produces sadness for the other, it increases our sensitivity towards the suffering of our fellow humans; and, if we are in a situation of conflict, it restores our peace by dissolving our desire for retaliation. If this peace is not authentic and deep, we cannot feel called to reconciliation because the natural impulse of us humans is to have the last word and the ruling hand over others. This deep peace that comes from Jesus occurs only after an authentic and profound conversion of the individual. This also translates into an attitude that Paul reveals in this way in his letter to the Galatians: "I have been crucified with Christ; and it is no longer I who live, but it is Christ who lives in me. And the life I now live in the flesh I live by faith in the Son of God, who loved me and gave himself for me" (Galatians 2:19–20).

It starts with recognizing in its correct perspective the internal reality of our emotions and desires; perceiving the greatness and perfection of God in his love for who we are. Also moderating the exaggerated love for oneself, that kind of egocentric love that forms a sort of secret kingdom of our egoism, where the entrance to authentic love for others is prevented.

A new blessedness

This new state of our relationships leads us to become aware of a humbler existence. Humble in that the storms and impulses of our worldly passions calm down, since our attention is not focused on our conveniences; rather, it is mediated by the presence of Jesus. And this experience is real. It is about being internally free to free others from our contempt and aggressive self-defense. We become the blessed, "Blessed are the pure in heart, for they will see God" (Matthew 5:8). This freedom brings us to a place beyond ourselves where we are able to see clearly a reality that does not reflect our own desires. We see a glimpse of Eden, recognizing the *shalom* God intended for all humanity.

By breaking down the barriers that prevented us from loving each other in a healthy way, we begin to love others in a process that can naturally lead first to an acceptance of human diversity. But with the empowerment of the Spirit of Christ, we then experience a different dimension of our attitude towards our neighbor: We begin to show mercy, to feel sorry for the other (not to have pity, which is a form of egocentrism where we feel superior), and finally, we give up competition against each other. What has happened is that we have changed the ego-centered model to a Christ-centered model, where there is no competition but compassion, affection, and solidarity.

This new attitude also leads us to face our discrepancies, gratuitous enmities, misunderstandings and adversities. All of these came from the model of dominance and competition that we have now renounced. Our new attitude is one of noncompetition, as well as inclusion, solidarity, affection, and humility.

The change is not magical, nor does it come suddenly as in a whirlwind of lights and heavenly rays. Rather, it requires an intimate connection with God through prayer, and a focused meditation on God's living Word: "Indeed, the word of God is living and active, sharper than any two-edged sword, piercing until it divides soul from spirit, joints from marrow; it is able to judge the thoughts and intentions of the heart" (Hebrews 4:12).

It is not about reading or studying the Bible, which is recommended and necessary. It is the simple reading of the Scriptures in silent meditation, in an attitude of prayer, silently waiting for what the Spirit of the Lord has to tell us.

This deeper reflection on human nature and God's calling is the flourishing of a new creation in an often hostile and self-ish world: "So if anyone is in Christ, there is a new creation: everything old has passed away; see, everything has become new!" (2 Corinthians 5:17). It is the present hope of *shalom* that we receive when we rely on God.

Additional aspects of perseverance in the paths of peace-making are to be humble, to be meek, and to live with a clean heart. Thus, the Beatitudes present at least partially, as in a kaleidoscope, important facets that are integrated into our pacifist purpose. Something similar occurs with the metaphor of the fruit of the Spirit that Paul speaks to the Galatians: var-ious aspects that seek to define something that is complex, and that complexity comes from being spiritually "organic." So it happens with the attitude and apostolate of reconciliation and keeping the peace: It is filled with life that the Spirit breathes in us. Therefore, peacemakers also have other qualities that emerge as blessings in their Christian walk, and that is the deep peace that comes from Jesus, lightens the world, and changes our relationships in favor of reconciliation and compassion.

. . . .
RESPONSE ESSAY

Pursuing Peace

▶ *Enock Shamapani, Choma, Zambia*

The BIC significantly emphasize *Pursuing Peace* as one of its core values. Jesus is the central figure in Christianity, and peace is firmly established in the teachings that are found in the New Testament.

In affirming peace, "We value all human life and promote forgiveness, understanding, reconciliation, and nonviolent resolution of conflict." Nevertheless, there are relational challenges affecting peace in Zambian society. On an individual level, violence toward women and children is prevalent, mostly manifesting in the form of defilement, rape, teen pregnancy, and early marriage. Socially, election fraud and land disputes often are resolved by using violence as a means to justice. Additionally, much of southern Africa struggles with the effects of climate change. Due to these changes, in Zambia we face water challenges and a shortage of grazing land. These scarcities produce conflict among our people and are not always resolved peacefully.

INDIVIDUAL AND SOCIAL RELATIONSHIPS

In Zambia, challenges to *Pursuing Peace* are caught up in our cultural narrative, where power is often manifest through physical punishment of the powerful over the powerless and where loyalty to family, clan, and tribe is elevated above all else. These realities impact our individual and social relationships. BIC Zambia is involved in education efforts to help create a positive peace witness.

Bringing peace to the home, a place where women are often subordinated with little power or dignity, is one way we seek peaceful relationships. Joining Village Savings-and-Loan Associations creates an environment where women are engaged as well as empowered. These local groups are an example of microfinance, giving women status in their family as income earners as well as supporting the economic development in their village. Women are also involved in local decision-making groups, such as parent-teacher committee and cooperative society. These examples show women that they are not only housekeepers but are also important beings in society who can foster sustainable development through peacebuilding.

Regarding children, the BIC churches in Zambia have started parenting education opportunities to help make parents aware of their roles and responsibilities to their children. Gatherings are arranged where both parents and children interact to share their experiences. Further, child protection policies have been developed in churches to protect children from many forms of abuse.

As a result of the recent (2022) corporal punishment ban in Zambian schools, peace clubs have become an integral part of extracurricular school programs. Started in 2006 through the work of Mennonite Central Committee, Peace Club Zambia now hosts thirty-two clubs across the country. The expressed hope is that when a child is educated early, it is easier for that child to practice what has been learned and pass the knowledge on to the next generation, thus breaking traditional patterns of exerting power. Participation in peace clubs teaches our children that peaceful resolution of conflict involves solving differences with tools such as dialogue, education, and knowledge.

On an individual level, peace calls for mental and emotional well-being, attributed to a sense of inner calmness and contentment. *Pursuing Peace* is a reflection of Jesus' nature and character, as expressed in John 14:27, "Peace I leave with you, my peace I give to you." Therefore, Christians are encouraged to receive Jesus' promise of shalom in order to have inner peace and strive for peace in all aspects of life.

PRACTICING PEACE

The dissonance between our dominant cultural influences related to power and loyalty and what we learn in Scripture about peace is strong. It is difficult to leave cultural privileges behind for the sake of following Jesus. We find hope in the teachings of Jesus, knowing they provide a foundational model for *Pursuing Peace*. In his Sermon on the Mount, Jesus says, "Blessed are the peacemakers, for they will be called children of God" (Matthew 5:9). This means that we are accountable for our actions and there are consequences when we do not seek peace.

Human nature is such that to show love to our enemies is thought to be a sign of weakness. However, Jesus taught his followers to love one another, and to love their enemies. He said, "You have heard that it was said, 'Love your neighbor and hate your enemy.' But I tell you, love your enemies and pray for those who persecute you" (Matthew 5:43–44 NIV). This practical demonstration of sincere love and forgiveness, even amidst an inevitable conflict, teaches us how to embrace Jesus' imperative toward peace.

We are called to live in unity and harmony. Romans 12:18 urges Christians to "live at peace with everyone." This passage encourages believers to actively seek peace and avoid actions that lead to conflict. Pastors often serve as mediators at the congregational level, called to speak biblical truth and offer Jesus-centered solutions to conflict resolution. Church leaders further teach peace at the congregational level through peace committees, which are allotted special Sundays to preach on the topic. Church women's groups are another place cultural norms are challenged in light of biblical truth. For instance, a young daughter-in-law may function almost as a slave in a traditional village setting. But Christian mothers-in-law encourage each other not to exercise this power but to treat these young women with kindness and love.

Teaching and encouraging believers in the importance of peace as a core value in the church is part of the transformation we experience when following Jesus. When a Christian has accepted Christ, they begin to experience spiritual peace alongside a sense in which we look forward to eternal peace with God. Through this transformation we embrace God's gift of shalom in our individual relationships and in our villages.

In conclusion, *Pursuing Peace* is a core value that aligns with the teaching of Jesus. Believers are called to actively work as peacemakers and negotiators of reconciliation. Our Christian tradition teaches us that responding to evil with good is a powerful way to pursue peace.

. . . .

RESPONSE ESSAY

Pursuing Peace

▶ *Zach Spidel, Dayton, Ohio*

Violence had never been an abstraction for Donald. It ran like a bright red thread through the warp and woof of his life. It was a tool to be used to protect himself and those he loved. It was a way to make things right, or as our chapter has it, a *means* to justice. At the same time, it was a threat to be feared and continually guarded against—a dark cloud under which he lived. Donald earned money on the side for his wife and kids by participating in illegal, unregulated fighting circles. He was built like a tank and usually won. After a set of threatening encounters on the street, he took to carrying a baseball bat with him on walks around the neighborhood I share with him on the east side of Dayton, Ohio.

One evening, while watching TV with his family, gunshots rang out just outside their street-level apartment. An instant later their front door was kicked in. His wife scooped up the kids and ran in terror to the back of the apartment. Donald jumped up ready to fight to the death, but the man who had kicked in his door collapsed onto the ground, blood seeping out of his gut. He had just been shot and in a fit of adrenaline-fueled desperation had managed to kick in the door of Donald's apartment in search of safety. Donald stood over the man, facing the door, his heart thumping, wondering if the shooter would be following him in. Thank God, he did not. When Donald recounted these events at our church, the Shepherd's Table (now East Dayton Fellowship) a few days later, he did so with a blank expression, his pain masked by flinty resolve.

When, as Donald's pastor, I spoke with him about Jesus' commands to love our enemies, turn the other cheek, and do good to those who harm us, we were not theorizing about fuzzy abstractions but confronting hard realities. Donald was attracted to this component of Jesus' message, but also skeptical. Even if, in theory, such a response to violence was what Jesus wanted, Donald doubted whether he could ever really react to another's aggression with love. Every muscle in his body called out, on such occasions, for a different response—how could he ever turn the other cheek? Only by the Spirit's power, I told him.

A practical test found Donald one Saturday afternoon in late summer on Second Street outside his mom's house. I had come by to remind the family of our Saturday evening service. Donald and his family are Black, as are most people on that block, yet the neighborhood is mostly made up of white people. Racial tensions in the neighborhood were real and Donald's brother, Marcus, and his brother's friend, Quentin, had been in an escalating conflict with a pair of white brothers from an intermittently homeless family down the road.

As I stood in the yard with Marcus and Quentin, those two white boys rode by on their bicycles with wicked grins on their faces. They had come to make trouble, whispering racial slurs as they rode by. My two teenage companions immediately tensed, fury written on their faces, their fingers curling reactively into fists. I called after the white boys, whom I also knew well, "Go home!" I knew where this was going.

They turned their bikes around at the end of the block and began riding back toward us and again let that racial epithet fly. I held up my hands to Marcus and Quentin, pleading with them not to respond to these verbal blows with physical ones. They held back. But once again the two white boys wheeled around and approached us. Before they could speak again, Marcus and Quentin tackled them off their bikes and a melee ensued. The younger white boy's nose was immediately smashed in, blood gushing onto his shirt. He, in particular, was physically overmatched and getting pummeled. I shielded him from worse by keeping myself between him and the others while pleading with all four to stop.

In an instant the scene resolved thus: The two white boys sitting bloodied on a curb on the far side of the street. Marcus and Quentin, relatively unscathed, standing furious in the street glaring past me at them. Donald and a crowd of family members and neighbors standing in the yard and growing angrier by the minute as the bloodied younger white boy kept yelling.

I was angry enough to want to hit him myself. I was also afraid. Donald's younger brother, Marcus, was being verbally assaulted with racial vitriol at his own home. I could see Donald tense and I knew what even a single blow from him could do to the racist kid bleeding freely from his nose onto the pavement below. I told that kid, "Shut up!"—which is not a formulation I usually use—and then I asked, perhaps a bit ridiculously, if anyone in that hastily assembled crowd had a cloth that might help staunch the kid's bleeding. A few faces went bug-eyed at the thought and a few choice words were yelled back. Donald turned quickly on his heels and disappeared back into the house. I wondered, and worried, what he might be going to get. Would it be that baseball bat?

He returned moments later with a washcloth which he had lightly wetted. Walking slowly across the street to the kid hurling epithets, he dropped the cloth into his lap. "Clean your face," he said, before he turned and joined me in the street. I was stunned by his act of boundary-crossing compassion.

I remain gratefully stunned still. I witnessed, in real time, the power of the Holy Spirit described for us in the anchor essay. The Spirit empowered Donald in that moment to break a barrier of hatred in order to offer an act of love. Rather than retaliate, the Spirit enabled him to offer an act of merciful compassion to one who was still demeaning him. Here was the power and character of God alive in the heart of my brother.

In a way that was costly and difficult and utterly beautiful, Donald listened to and followed Jesus in blessing his enemy that day. The Spirit alive in Donald made it possible for him to live in step with Jesus even though doing so cut against the grain of his flesh. He wanted to punch the mouth that uttered those hateful words, but instead he offered help to one who uttered them. In doing so, Donald became for me a living example of the nonviolent way of Jesus. I thank God for my brother and hope that we BIC might live up to the embodied example of Christ's enemy love he displayed that day.

. . . .
CHAPTER 8

Discussion Questions

1. Among the different values that define the BIC profile, how does the search for peace and reconciliation affect your life and your home?

2. In the Jesus saying of John 14:27, how would you compare peace from the world and peace from Jesus? Try to describe both from present-day life.

3. Can you point out which aspects of human justice contradict Jesus' call for peace and reconciliation?

4. Nationalism is frequently at the root of war. Share ideas in the group about how nationalism could be moderated by the message of peace and reconciliation from our tradition.

5. Time to share more intimately: How do you deepen your spirituality, preventing religion from being just culture?

Living Simply

Scott MacFeat and Ryan Stockton

*We value uncluttered lives, which free us to
love boldly, give generously, and serve joyfully.*

INTRODUCTION

My (Ryan) family used to live in Brooklyn, New York. During
that time, we lived in some pretty small apartments. After New
York we moved to New Jersey and lived in a small town in a
small townhouse. Now we are in suburban Pennsylvania, and
we live in the biggest house we have ever had. Compared to
many in the United States, the house is a modest home from
the early 1970s, yet compared to the rest of the world it is
quite large. But sometimes I wonder: In choosing this house,
did we decide against living simply? Have we opted for comfort and luxury over simplicity?

The answer to these questions might be yes *if* we defined
living simply as the size of our houses or the number of possessions we own. But is that really what *Living Simply* is
all about? The BIC has defined *Living Simply* as "valu(ing)
uncluttered lives, which free us to love boldly, give generously,

and serve joyfully."[1] Clearly, we have more in mind than just our physical possessions.

Defining what *Living Simply* means can be difficult when what constitutes simplicity changes from context to context and culture to culture. What is considered simple in suburban Pennsylvania might be different from what is considered simple in Zambia.

Interpreting the *Living Simply* value is *not* attempting to make moralistic pronunciations about people and their choices individually. The *Living Simply* value ought not be interpreted with a legalistic lens. For example, cluttered personal spaces such as homes or offices do not make us "bad Christians" regarding this value. Cultivating simple living is not accomplished through shame, but rather, is framed in freedom. Many of us, for a variety of reasons, find simplicity unattainable or difficult. But when we approach simplicity as a means for freeing us for mission, God invites us to holy minimalism for the sake of the kingdom (Matthew 6:33).

A POSTURE OF SIMPLE LIVING

As my wife and I (Ryan) think about the various obligations in our lives, we are careful to not *should* ourselves. When we *should* all of the time, we end up feeling guilty and end up more tired and guilt-ridden than we need to be. We must be careful when it comes to considering this core value: "I should be less messy," "I should have fewer things," and so on. When taking this posture, we tread the line of shame. In affirming that we value *Living Simply*, we are merely saying that practicing this value, to whatever degree we can, provides us an opportunity for spiritual growth, not rightness or wrongness.

The above-mentioned examples refer to messy personal spaces and physical things. But this value encompasses far more than physical possessions or clutter. It goes beyond attempting minimalism and instead moves to a posture of the heart that touches all aspects of our lives.

In his book, *Praying Like Monks, Living Like Fools*, author Tyler Staton talks about the posture of Jesus, who was intentional in his time with the Father, yet in that intentionality, still allowed himself to be interrupted for the sake of other people. Stanton says "There's a word for that posture: *unhurried*. Hurry is the great enemy of the spiritual life. Why? Because hurry kills love."[2]

An unhurried posture is one result of *Living Simply*. When we are living uncluttered lives, we are freed to love boldly as Jesus did, to give generously as Jesus did, and to serve joyfully as Jesus did. And what *uncluttered* looks like will vary from person to person. But we are looking for the posture of Jesus, who lived a simple life and in so doing was free from the demands of others on his life and schedule, free from the slavery of possessions and money, and free to be able to love more fully and presently. As we obediently *Follow Jesus*, another BIC core value, this freedom leads to our ability to love, give, and serve better.

Living Simply in the Scripture

No text readily speaks to *Living Simply*. However, there is a posture found throughout the Scriptures. One could look at passages such as Proverbs 30:8, Colossians 3:1–3, 1 Timothy 6:6–10, or Hebrews 13:5 to help paint a picture. The writings of Paul also provide an overarching approach to simplicity when he urges the Philippian churches to "live your life in a manner worthy of the gospel of Christ" (Philippians 1:27a). But what does that mean?

Let us first consider the fact that Paul was in prison when he wrote these words. Historians know that the first century prison system within the Roman Empire was not accommodating to basic human needs. For instance, in Philippians 1:13, Paul mentions that he is "in chains for Christ" (NIV). His imprisonment in the governor's palace indicates that this was a type of military imprisonment. Because of that, it is possible Paul was chained to an imperial soldier rather than to a wall, since this was a common practice. If that is the case, then any "significant physical movement" from Paul would have required permission from the guard.[3]

Still, whether he was chained to a wall or a guard, Paul was stripped of any ability to help himself. Therefore it was up to his family and friends to provide for his needs. This is why he was thankful to the Philippian church for sending provisions with his brother in Christ, Epaphroditus (Philippians 4:18).

And so, as a prisoner, Paul was dependent on others. Yet he could still say, "I have learned to be content with whatever I have. I know what it is to have little, and I know what it is to have plenty. In any and all circumstances I have learned the secret of being well-fed and of going hungry, of having plenty and of being in need. I can do all things through him who strengthens me" (Philippians 4:11b-13).

This posture of contentedness is at the heart of *Living Simply*. It is a posture that reflects a life lived for the gospel of Christ. Furthermore, it stood in stark contrast to the first century Greco-Roman culture.

Aristotle, a fourth century BC ancient Greek philosopher, shaped much of the moral philosophy that pervaded the Greco-Roman civilization during the time Paul lived. His definition of contentment was "possessing all things and needing nothing."[4] In other words, being completely self-reliant was held in high regard; not unlike today's Western culture. Arguably, contentedness in the twenty-first century continues to be a contrast to a cultural emphasis on capitalism and individualism.

But Paul inverts this cultural value from Aristotle. He says that "whatever gains I had, these I have come to regard as loss because of Christ. More than that, I regard everything as loss because of the surpassing value of knowing Christ Jesus my Lord" (Philippians 3:7–8a). Rather than relishing his own accomplishments and possessions, he considers them all worthless when compared to the richness that is found in knowing Jesus.

It is easy to imagine Paul in chains, on his knees, meditating on the first line of Psalm 23: "The Lord is my shepherd, I shall not want." This is the posture of living a simple life worthy of the gospel and the advancement of the kingdom. It is recognizing that, no matter where we are from, we need to learn how to depend on Jesus in every situation. We know from the BIC core value *Relying on God* to respond to God in a way that is not self-reliant.

In fact, Paul says that he has "learned to be content" (Philippians 4:11). That learning is a process, and it is continual and ongoing. It is the sum of our experiences that help us realize what truly matters in life.

Paul's motivation for gospel advancement was what helped him have the capacity to be content in all situations. It was this posture that helped him learn the value of *Living Simply* so that others could be blessed. The same is true for the church today. *Living Simply* is a posture that the church can take as we practice godliness with contentment for the glory of God and for the building of his kingdom.

PERSONAL CONSIDERATIONS

Paul wrote, "There is great gain in godliness combined with contentment" (1 Timothy 6:6), but contentment does not equal complacency. Every follower of Jesus has a part to play. Each of us has tasks that God prepared in advance for us to do (Ephesians 2:10). Again, at the heart of learning to be content is the value of *Living Simply* for the sake of advancing the gospel.

Personally, this might mean taking a hard look at your calendar. Is there anything in your schedule that involves the mission of advancing the message of Jesus? That is a good question, but it is also kind of a trick question because as Christians, we represent Jesus everywhere we go, no matter what we are doing. God does not need time blocked out on our calendar so that we can fit him in. He is in all of it.

In this case, keeping an eternal perspective with everything we do is one way to approach simple living. It is not an insignificant perspective when we realize that we are meant to live every moment for the One who is King of all our moments. This does not mean that we cannot enjoy activities like going to an amusement park or seeing a concert, but we do them knowing that our joy is made more complete through the presence of God with us and knowing that we can be the presence of God to others in those moments.

CORPORATE CONSIDERATIONS

We have the opportunity to rethink how we approach simplicity corporately in the church. By exploring elements of church practice that invite us to lean into the freedom found in simple living, we can develop healthy practices related to tithing and sabbath rest. While the dominant cultural narrative we often hear tells us that tithing is a burden and that rest hinders productivity, the lens of simple living offers an alternative. This alternative narrative, as we will see, demonstrates a reframing of position rooted in the abundance and goodness of God toward his creation.

Giving generously

Freedom found in *Living Simply* can impact our practice of tithing. Some of us live in a culture where anytime the local congregation discusses money, everyone seems to hold their breath. It is a topic that can feel invasive when it is preached from the pulpit because the cultural nuance invites us to think that tithing is a personal choice and not a biblical act of obedience.

Not all congregations face this challenge. And no matter what part of the world we live in, as followers of Christ, we can affirm when David says, "The earth is the LORD's and all that is in it, the world, and those who live in it" (Psalm 24:1). David's mindset was simple: Everything he had was the Lord's.

Our culture teaches us a narrative of scarcity. Daily, we are drawn into the myth that we do not have enough and should safeguard what we do have. We see evidence in the Old Testament, however, that God creates, not from scarcity, but from a place of generosity. Theologian Walter Brueggemann suggests we adopt a "liturgy of abundance" rather than operating from a mindset of scarcity.[5] He uses the Exodus story to show how the Israelites are freed from the demands of Pharoah and are taught to rely on God. Today, as we rely on God and root ourselves in abundance, we are free to give generously because we know that the Lord will use our gifts for his glory, no matter the size.

Sabbath living

Another consideration for *Living Simply* is the practice of sabbath rest. The concept of rest in the Bible is rooted in Genesis 2 in the Garden of Eden. After God had finished Creation, he rested on the seventh day. The Hebrew word for rest is *sabat*, or sabbath. We typically think of resting as a time on our calendar that we designate for inactivity. But, as one BIC pastor asks, based on Genesis 2, what if biblical rest "is a way of life grounded in the goodness of God?"[6]

The author of Hebrews says it this way: "So then, a sabbath rest still remains for the people of God; for those who enter God's rest also cease from their labors as God did from his. Let us therefore make every effort to enter that rest" (Hebrews 4:9–11). The author is not talking about Christians practicing a Jewish Sabbath. Rather, entering God's sabbath rest involves actively participating in the works of God.

Practically speaking, sabbath rest is not about collapsing on the sofa and binge watching your favorite TV show all day. Biblical rest involves nourishing your soul as we celebrate and participate with God's will. New Testament scholar Dr. Donald A. Hagner writes:

> "[Sabbath] is essentially a day of celebration, a time of happiness, feasting, and spiritual joy, and at the same time a rejoicing in God's creation and an anticipation of final. . . fulfillment. Thus it points forward to, and tastes in advance, [a future and ultimate] *shalom* ("peace"): ultimate well-being in every regard, the time when redemption is fully and finally realized."[7]

When we enter into sabbath rest, we are not only accomplishing the works God has prepared for us, but we are enriching our spiritual well-being. Joining as the body of Christ and participating in things that build our faith expresses the love of Jesus with the world around us.

A SIMPLE FAITH

A simple faith is best understood as being unprogrammed, obedient, and salvation minded. It is not meant as a synonym for having a lack of intelligence, nor is it something done easily or simply. Rather, when we are confident of God's provision over our lives we can focus on following Jesus. When we do this, we are extended a divine invitation so we can freely love, give, and serve.

Doing vs. being

As a Christian who grew up in the United States, I (Scott) instinctively want to program outcomes. I remember when I worked in a commercial business, I felt called to talk about Jesus with my coworkers. This usually led to great conversations, but I wanted to take it a step further. My desire was to fulfill the great commission by making disciples who make disciples. So, I eagerly invited my coworkers to an early morning Bible study at the local coffee shop. We decided to meet once per week to discuss a predetermined passage, complete with my own discussion questions. But after only a couple meetings, I quickly realized I was overcomplicating things.

In this example, discipleship does not only equal Bible study. Discipleship involves building relationships. It is about integrating and sharing life with your neighbors as you speak and model the gospel. It is about praying with and for those we sit next to in church. It is about being slow to speak and quick to listen as you show the love of Jesus (James 1:19).

Our emphasis on producing outcomes is, at its core, a doing approach to faith. In his *Emotionally Healthy* series, Peter Scazzero shifts our focus from doing (for God) to being (with God) in our approach to faith. Scazzero says, "We must flee from a life of overcommitment and hurry in order to learn how to *be before we do*."[8] Notice how simplicity is implied in Scazzero's comment.

God can certainly use our efforts in programming, but sometimes he calls us to release our preconceived outcomes and rely on him to lead our conversations and interactions with people. There is a freedom in allowing God to work and use us without our own overplanned agendas weighing us down.

Simple does not necessarily imply unplanned and disordered. Simple can be intentional and focused. Ultimately, simple focuses on being before doing.

Obediently following Jesus

But what about a simple faith regarding obedience? Obedience that the Lord desires is not a blind, dispassionate, or robotic obedience (Isaiah 29:13).

Consider when Jesus was challenged by the Pharisees and teachers of the law. They were upset that the disciples did not wash their hands before they ate, which was according to their tradition. Jesus responded to them by saying, "Isaiah was right when he prophesied about you hypocrites; as it is written: 'These people honor me with their lips, but their hearts are far from me. They worship me in vain; their teachings are merely human rules'" (Mark 7:6–7 NIV).

Jesus was illustrating that God wants our hearts, not vain obedience. Simple obedience looks like someone who believes (Genesis 15:6), someone who trusts (Proverbs 3:5–6), and someone who does what the Word of God says out of a loyal love for him (James 1:22; 1 John 4:19).

Salvation minded

A simple faith is salvation minded. In other words, rather than dwelling on insignificant and historically debatable doctrines, what if we only cling tightly to the larger tenets of our faith? This is often described as the difference between salvation issues and secondary issues.

Sometimes these secondary issues will be theological, but sometimes they will be cultural. Here in the United States, our political affiliations are sometimes elevated to primary importance and complicate our faith, e.g., the concept of Christian nationalism. Elsewhere it could be tribal loyalties, familial loyalties, or cultural expectations of men and women. The possibilities are endless. That is not to say that these areas cannot be important to us, but having a simple faith can help us differentiate between these cultural issues and the salvation issues.

An uncluttered faith could look like holding tightly to things like the life, death, and resurrection of Jesus, the trinitarian understanding of the Godhead, the purpose of the church, loving God and our neighbors, making disciples who make disciples, etc. As we keep a tight grip on these core issues with one hand, the other hand remains open, inviting in Christian love further discussions on the non-core issues of our faith. This posture of *Living Simply* in our faith is what frees us to love others boldly even when we disagree.

SIMPLE RELATIONSHIPS

As anyone can attest, relationships can be messy. All of us have experienced misunderstandings, disagreements, and some of us even outright betrayal on our journeys with other people.

1 Corinthians 13:4–5 tells us "Love is patient; love is kind; love is not envious or boastful or arrogant or rude. It does not insist on its own way; it is not irritable; it keeps no record of wrongs. . ." (NRSVue). When we are keeping a record of wrongs, our relationships can get complicated. We will

inevitably find ourselves offended or hurt in some way. If we let those dictate the rest of our relationships, we would soon find ourselves isolated and alone, sitting in our resentments.

Forgiveness

Forgiveness is an important factor in building relationships. Learning to forgive, which itself is the subject of many other books, is imperative when it comes to uncomplicating our relationships. But this value speaks to more than just our forgiveness of others. When you offend someone else, you can own up to it, take responsibility, and work to make it right with the other person. In doing this, you help them to have an uncomplicated relationship with you.

The desired outcome in forgiveness is reconciliation and a movement toward biblical *shalom*. As BIC we also value *Pursuing Peace* in our relationships with others. When we find ourselves in moments of conflict our tendency might not be to pursue peace. Healthy dialogue can help us forgive. In *Peaceful Practices*, a curriculum of the Mennonite Central Committee, we are encouraged to dialogue:

> In part, we dialogue because it is faithful. We also dialogue because it creates change. Conversations and vulnerable storytelling have the possibility of changing hearts and minds, a fundamental and constant ambition of the Christian life. We are working to build the kingdom of God on earth, following Christ's example.[9]

Integrity

Personal integrity can keep our relationships simple as well. Lying or putting on a mask in front of others can be exhausting when you must constantly keep track of who thinks what, what you have told others, etc. We cannot control how others relate to us, but when we forgive others, tell the truth consistently, when we keep short accounts, we save much of the energy and anxiety of maintaining difficult and complicated relationships.

This can also help us as we think about the area of addictions. Addictions can clutter and complicate a life exponentially. Secrets are kept to hide one's attachments and issues, lies are told to maintain unhealthy habits, relational resentments feed the addictions, anxieties and insecurities continually drive people to their coping mechanisms. Addictions complicate and strangle a life of joy and freedom.

To the extent that we can work toward simple relationships, uncluttered by secrets, records of wrongs committed, or whatever mess we allow to fester, we can then be freed to love others boldly, give of ourselves to others generously, and serve others joyfully.

LIVING SIMPLY AND TECHNOLOGY

The internet has helped to bring access to information and global communication, which can be a good thing. But technology does not always simplify our lives.

The internet, especially social media, tends to have an adverse effect on our desire to live simply. In fact, social media is designed with the intention to keep us coming back to check our notifications and keep us scrolling. Dr. Nicholas Kardaras, in his book *Digital Madness*, notes that "Tech is designed to increasingly tickle our dopamine and leave us hungry for more. . . . But like any addiction, there's never enough."[10]

Therefore, what seems like minutes on our screens add up to hours as we are bombarded with the overwhelming message that our life could be better. Our constant intake of social media, games, movies, television, and newsfeeds all work in tandem to shape our minds toward the cultural priorities of consumerism and consumption that surround us, rather than Christ and his kingdom.

Therein lies the most pressing issue: Being addicted to technology has both physical and spiritual consequences. One of the many modern ways Satan and his spiritual forces lead the world astray is through the misuse and overuse of technology (Revelation 12:9). It is a strategy that tempts us to align our desires with the ads on our phones rather than the desires of Jesus. When that happens, the fear that our hearts will be consumed by what we possess is eclipsed by the fear of not having what everyone else has (Matthew 6:21).

However, our smartphones, the internet, and other technology can be helpful tools. But if we are not diligent in our usage, it will rob us of our ability to love boldly, give generously, or serve joyfully because we are turned inward. So much of what we see online is designed to turn us toward consumption and a lack of contentment. When our desires begin to line up with the desires of the world, we become blind to those around us and numbed to a biblical selflessness that enables us to love, give, and serve others.

FREED TO LOVE, GIVE, AND SERVE

How can we know or measure if we are *Living Simply*? How can we know if our lives are uncluttered enough? As previously discussed, a precise definition will not be possible given our variety of experiences and contexts. But we can find some guidance in the wording of the core value itself: being freed to love boldly, give generously, and serve joyfully.

If we are hindered in our pursuit of any of these things, we might have some uncluttering to do; perhaps more simplicity could benefit us. In her article "Quaker Reflections on Simplicity," Eileen Kinch says "Simplicity is setting aside anything that gets in the way of seeking the Kingdom."[11] So, do we have relationships that need to be freed from grudges, resentments, or unrealistic expectations so that we can love boldly? Maybe loving boldly is the way we can make relationships simple, by not indulging in the mess of anger or immaturity.

Perhaps we do not have many physical possessions, but we have a longing for them. Sometimes the desire for more or for something different can be just as distracting for us as the things themselves.

Maybe our calendars are so packed that we have no time or energy to give to a neighbor or friend or family member. Are we so constantly on the go that whenever we do eventually find time to give to someone, we aren't fully present because we're always thinking about the next thing, the next place to be, or our next obligation?

We must be aware of our internet and social media usage. If our smart devices demand so much of our time and attention that we have nothing to give to others and we forget to attend to things that really matter, then the distraction is a barrier to freedom. Do we find it difficult to love boldly, give generously, or serve joyfully? Are there barriers to us having the unhurried posture of Jesus or the content posture of Paul? How might we be distracted from living in these ways? If so, where could we simplify to free ourselves toward these aspirations?

As another of our core values states, we want to be a people committed to *Following Jesus*. He was on a mission and had purpose, yet was unhurried. He was never distracted from loving people in whatever ways they needed to be loved. That is what this value is ultimately about: Being free to love people better.

• • • • • • • • • • • • • • • •

RESPONSE ESSAY

Living Simply

▶ *Warren Hoffman, Elizabethtown, Pennsylvania*

The word *affluenza* is a blend of two words, *affluence* and *influenza*. This melded word was devised to describe the detrimental effects of materialism. *Merriam-Webster's Unabridged Dictionary* defines affluenza as "the pursuit of wealth and success. . . resulting in a life of chronic dissatisfaction, debt, overwork, stress, and impaired relationships."

Two millennia ago, the apostle Paul issued a stiff warning against this scourge, writing that even a hint of affluenza is improper for God's holy people (Ephesians 5:3). Jesus was even more forceful. He warned, "Any one of you who does not renounce all that he has cannot be my disciple" (Luke 14:33 ESV). He also matched this warning with an extraordinary promise: "Truly I tell you, there is no one who has left house or brothers or sisters or mother or father or children or fields, for my sake and for the sake of the good news, who will not receive a hundredfold now in this age—houses, brothers and sisters, mothers and children, and fields, with persecutions— and in the age to come eternal life" (Mark 10:29–30).

This surprising combination of relinquishment and reward is at the heart of *Living Simply.* Uncluttered lives open the way for the freedom of contentment, the joy of generosity, and the confidence of purposeful living.

LIBERATING CONTENTMENT

As an example of contentment, Paul gave this testimony: "I have learned to be content with whatever I have. I know what it is to have little, and I know what it is to have plenty"

(Philippians 4:11–12). Paul had no need to gather and stock-pile resources to protect his comfort and security. He could be serene with much or little because he was certain that God would care for his basic needs. He assured the Philippians: "And my God will fully satisfy every need of yours according to his riches in glory in Christ Jesus" (Philippians 4:19).

My wife, Connie, and I were the beneficiaries of such rad-ical contentment during our first ministry assignment in a disadvantaged community on the outskirts of Salem, Oregon. The only realistic option for housing in that community was to purchase a small, one-bedroom house. With the interven-tion of our bishop, we were able to secure a loan. Without any resources of our own, however, we could not manage the down payment.

At that point, college friends, John and Esther Spurrier, offered to loan us the full down payment with no interest. They said that as a resident physician, "John is earning money, more than we need. Use these funds as long as necessary and return them when you can." With this posture of contentment and generosity, already in the early years of their marriage, it is no wonder that the Spurriers went on to give nearly three decades of faithful service in full-time medical missions at Macha Mission Hospital in Zambia.

For John and Esther, a biblical standard of living can be summed up in a single word: enough. Having enough and resting in the assurance that God will provide all they need, they have been able to freely give money and time in caring for others.

JOYFUL GENEROSITY

The apostle Paul affirms Macedonian Christians who, in extreme poverty themselves, joyfully gave more than they could afford, beyond their ability, to help believers in Jerusalem pressed by famine (2 Corinthians 8:1–5). With this daring generosity in mind, Paul writes, "The one who sows sparingly will also reap sparingly, and the one who sows bountifully will also reap bountifully" (2 Corinthians 9:6).

Jesus was even more emphatic: "Give, and it will be given to you. A good measure, pressed down, shaken together, running over, will be put into your lap; for the measure you give will be the measure you get back" (Luke 6:38).

Amid unrelenting increases in the costs of living, we may not yet be giving a full 10 percent tithe to our home congregation. To start this practice may seem reckless—until we experience for ourselves how God provides. Then, with reenforced faith, we can dare to give even more generously.

God entrusts all of us with time, talent, and treasure. When we cheerfully share what we have, in poverty or wealth, we will always have enough of everything, and can share abundantly in every good work (2 Corinthians 9:6–8).

PURPOSEFUL LIVING

The sinful core of affluenza in our acquisitive cultures is the dogged pursuit of money. The antidote is a wholehearted pursuit of the purposes of God. Jesus said, "But seek first the kingdom of God and his righteousness, and all these things will be added to you" (Matthew 6:33 ESV). When we devote ourselves to the purposes of God, our work, whatever it is, becomes an assignment by God to serve others. Though we may receive compensation, our work becomes a calling from God (1 Corinthians 7:17).

Money and possessions take their proper place lower on our list of priorities. We no longer ask: "How can I make the most money?" Instead, we ask: "How, with my abilities and opportunities, can I be of greatest service to God and others?"

When questions of lifestyle arise, we can answer them in light of our assignment from God. By this measure, we are not bound by an arbitrary set of rules. We need not compare ourselves with others. Rather, in obedience to Jesus, we can decide what is necessary and what is excess by the requirements of our calling. As God reorders our priorities, we can recalibrate our pace to free time for others. Even amid full schedules, we honor our time for worship and sabbath rest.

As we simplify our lives, intentionally in our particular circumstances, we will experience for ourselves a joyful fusion of relinquishment and reward. In his essay "The Weight of Glory," C. S. Lewis offers this penetrating insight:

> The New Testament has a lot to say about self-denial, but not about self-denial as an end in itself. We are told to deny ourselves and take up our crosses in order that we may follow Christ; and to nearly every description of what we shall ultimately find if we do so contains an appeal to desire. . . . Indeed, if we consider the unblushing promises of reward and the staggering nature of the rewards promised in the Gospel, it would seem that Our Lord finds our desire not too strong, but too weak.

In response to Jesus' teaching and example, and the witness of the New Testament, the BIC value uncluttered lives, which free us to love boldly, give generously, and serve joyfully.

. . . .

RESPONSE ESSAY

Living Simply

▶ *Levison Soko, Lusaka, Zambia*

As a pastor in BIC Church-Zambia Conference, I had the privilege of buying a smartphone, which had the features I was looking for to assist me with schoolwork. One member must have checked the price of the phone; she came and jokingly asked me, "Pastor, is that simple living?"

Living Simply is one of the most challenging of the BIC core values to interpret, mostly because it depends greatly on how simplicity is understood. While the value is interpreted and lived out differently across cultures, broad application of the value shows us that simple living results in our individual and corporate ability to love, give, and serve.

FREEDOM FROM SELF

The essay argues that to gain the freedom to love, give, and serve, we must acknowledge and address our cluttered spiritual lives. I agree with Eileen Kinch, who comments, "Simplicity is setting aside anything that gets in the way of seeking the Kingdom."[12] All the materials I possess are a gift from God. So when I consider the postures of simple living associated with this value, I need to adopt the attitude of a steward. For me and other believers to practice and value uncluttered lives, we must die to self for the sake of the Kingdom. The Lord of lords and the King of kings is calling us to be his disciples so that our lives bring eternal reward, glorify God, and serve others. We have the capacity to choose life or death, to obey God or Satan, to walk under obedience to either our own desires or the desires of Jesus.

When we act according to our self-interest we cannot truly respond to God's call on our life. Therefore, dying to self means denying an attitude of self-seeking and egoism, surrendering our dreams, plans, goals, and wealth into God's will. In doing this we live for Jesus, as Paul pronounces, "Count yourselves dead to sin but alive to God in Christ Jesus" (Romans 6:11 NIV).

In short, the shedding of self requires that we daily submit to the will of God. Only through the empowerment of the Holy Spirit can this be done. Every decision made and every word spoken should be approached with a constant awareness that we are to live worthy of the calling (Ephesians 4:1–2). Dying to self will keep us humble and allow us to be open to reach out to others in the community. In the book of Acts, we can be in such awe and wonder at the faithfulness of the disciples that we may think it is impossible to live in such a way. When truly living under the lordship of Christ, we must learn to die to ourselves daily, and we must live with a compassion that reaches out to people in our villages and cities.

SIMPLICITY IN RELATIONSHIPS

BIC Zambia consists of congregations in rural and urban settings, and both contexts provide an opportunity for our people to demonstrate the value of simple relationships. When there is a funeral in the neighborhood, I do not wait to be invited and asked what to do. Rather, as people who live in the same village or city, we gather ourselves at the funeral house, sleep there and help with whatever work needs to be done. For example, ladies will be cooking and drawing water while the men will be busy with burial preparations. As Africans, we believe in the spirit of Ubuntu, and affirm the principle *I am because you are*. As people we are connected, and we depend on one other.

A POSTURE OF SIMPLICITY

Outside the bounds of Christianity, humanity tends to live and act as if we humans are the true owners of everything we possess. Lacking eternal perspective, our sole ambition is seemingly to gain wealth on earth, allowing money to be our false god. When we come to faith, affirming that everything we have belongs to God and that he made everything for his glory (Genesis 1), we better understand that we cannot serve two masters: we cannot serve both God and money (Matthew 6:19–24). At the forefront of a posture of simplicity is an attentiveness to how we use and manage our possessions and resources. By asking, "What's my attitude toward everything God has given?" we are re-centered and able to receive and be content.

In 2019, Zambia did not receive enough rain, hence our crops were greatly affected, and we had a very poor harvest. We had to train our greedy eyes away from keeping our staple food, maize, to ourselves. My house had several visitors daily, church members and non–church members. My family was not spared from the shortage, but out of love, we found it a joy to serve others and share generously with them. This spirit, or attitude, that my family demonstrated spread to other church members who were then willing to share with other villagers. Paul himself prays that the eyes of our understanding may be enlightened to see the things that others cannot see (Ephesians 1:15–23).

We must appreciate the need to give our time, abilities, and material possessions to others when the Lord directs. It is my conviction that the gifts from God are to be used in his service for the benefit of all humankind. "Each of you should use whatever gift you have received to serve others, as faithful stewards of God's grace in its various forms" (1 Peter 4:10 NIV). Slowly,

I am seeing myself and people in my community doing the hard work to free ourselves from uncluttered lives by loving boldly, giving generously, and serving joyfully.

. . . .

CHAPTER 9

Discussion Questions

1. What are the cultural messages that surround you where you live and how might they be contrary to this core value of *Living Simply*?

2. In regard to having a simple faith, in what ways have you seen the church harmed by elevating issues of lesser importance to positions of greatest importance? How might stressing a simple faith benefit the church?

3. Which of the three areas of loving boldly, giving generously, and serving joyfully would you like to grow in over the next year?

4. Think through your calendar, your possessions, your relationships, your religious life. . . . What barriers are there to loving boldly, giving generously, and serving joyfully in your life?

5. Sometimes our desires align more with "the ads on our phones rather than the desires of Jesus." What are some practical steps you can take to be more aware of and resist worldly desires?

CHAPTER 10

Relying on God

Joshua Nolt

We confess our dependence on God for everything, and seek to deepen our intimacy with him by living prayerfully.

INTRODUCTION

What we rely on God for is where our minds can easily go when we think of this value of *Relying on God*. For protection. For strength. For money. For healing. For workers. For a building. For food. The list could go on and on, varying from congregation to congregation, country to country, and context to context.

Thinking about this value with an emphasis on what we are relying on God for could easily turn into a comparison game between local and global churches of who is relying on God more, depending on what they are relying on God for. Unintentionally, the emphasis on *for* creates a pecking order, whereby we try to measure who has more or less faith. Those with great faith are relying on God for bigger things, or perhaps those with greater faith are receiving what they are relying on God for.

This essay seeks to understand *Relying on God* as a response—a response to who God is and what God is doing. Our response to God comes through growing into our identity as children of God. This is not our natural disposition, and so first we will think about ways we relate to God that challenge our growth into this childlike identity. We will then follow this with a gospel story presenting an invitation to receive our identity as God's children, and then explore two historical practices of the church, communion and prayer, which invite us to experience this identity.

CHALLENGES TO *RELYING ON GOD*

Depending on our context, *Relying on God* can be replaced with reliance on whatever it is our culture values and emphasizes. In Western contexts, since the time of the Protestant Reformation, there has been a slow but deliberate emphasis on the individual, which has placed the weight of reliance on the self. Other cultures place a greater emphasis on family or the community. All contexts must reckon with how their particular culture's source of reliance takes the place of God.

In an American context, over the past several decades the church has looked to the corporate world to guide its understanding of leadership and structure. Efficient leaders and top-down structures have shaped expectations of leadership and how to run an organization. In some cases, these methods have produced large congregations whose size, scope, and reach have communicated images of success, which have then become the expectation of churches of all sizes in many cultures and contexts. What is being uncovered, in churches large and small who have adopted such methodology, is how much this approach really centered on us and not God.

Luke Keefer Jr. calls out such patterns in the church, saying,

It seems that a church without the Spirit sees all problems as a structural issue. If somehow, we change the administrative furniture, switch to a new program for outreach, select different people for leadership, or call the ultimate conference on evangelism, then "presto," we are bound to have success. . . . The changing we most need is in ourselves through the supply of the Spirit of the Lord. Until that crucial change happens, all we are doing with our committees, councils, conferences, and programs is merely casting lots on the luck of human personnel. Our better sense tells us the issue is deeper.[1]

Keefer helps ask the question: "What have we come to rely on that has taken the place of God?" This is a question of means. How we go about something is just as important as what it is we want to achieve. If the character of how we go about something is disconnected from the character of Jesus, it suggests what we are relying on is something other than God.

Parker Palmer calls this practice of replacing God functional atheism. He says functional atheism is "the belief that ultimate responsibility for everything rests with us. This is the unconscious, unexamined conviction that if anything decent is going to happen here, we are the ones who must make it happen—a conviction held even by people who talk a good game about God."[2]

Notice the words "unconscious and unexamined." The air of disbelief or functional atheism has become so normalized it takes effort to discern our motives and methods. Serving as a pastor in the American church for over twenty years, it has been my experience that the philosophies of leadership, structure, and strategy are entangled and intertwined with the values of my culture, with a capitalist and consumerist

approach to life. As you examine your own context, what
might you discover you have learned to rely on that is unconscious and unexamined?

PERSONAL CHALLENGES TO *RELYING ON GOD*

So what is *Relying on God*? Jesus tells a story that helps us
understand—what it is, and what it is not.

In Luke 15, Jesus tells a familiar story: the parable of the
lost sons. This parable uncovers a common, unexamined way
of relating to God. It also gives us a foundation of what it
means to rely on God in the best of ways.

An invitation to receive

A father has two sons. The younger one, perhaps a bit ambi-
tious and precocious, asks his father for his share of the inheritance. The father grants the request, and the son sets about
on a rampage of youthful revelry. Eventually, the money runs
out and he finds himself feeding alongside the unclean swine.
He has a thought: "My father's servants have it better than
this!" He thinks of what he will tell his father when he returns.
"Father, I have sinned against heaven and against you. I am no
longer worthy to be called your son; make me like one of your
hired servants" (Luke 15:18–19 NIV).

Notice how the younger son thinks his sonship is based on
what he has done. Notice how easily he severs his relationship
as his father's son, and how readily he is willing to take on the
identity of a servant.

Being a servant is easier than being a son. If you move from
being a son to being a servant, your father moves from being
your parent to being your boss. If he is now your boss, then
your worth is now based on performance. Performance is
based on you. You earn your worth.

This son has performed poorly as a son—and so now he wants to be treated as a servant. He wants to try harder and earn his value. The same pride that drove him to demand his inheritance and spend it how he wished is fueling his place as a servant in his father's house.

This son has not changed a bit. He may return, but his identity has not changed. The son is still in control. He was in control when he asked for his inheritance. He was in control when he spent the money and how he wanted to spend it. He is in control again as he defines the new arrangement. As a servant he will be able to make up for what he has done and prove his worth to his father. The son has yet to learn what it is to be a son of the father in this story.

And he is not the only one.

Toward the end of the story, we are introduced to the older brother—the one who stayed home and performed his duties faithfully. After a day of labor spent in the field, he returns home to the sound of music and laughter. His brother has returned home, a party has been thrown, and this brother refuses to enter. The father exits the party and "pleads" with the older son to join. The son responds, "Look! All these years I've been slaving for you and never disobeying your orders. You never even let me have a small party with a few of my friends! But this son of yours comes home after blowing your money on prostitutes, and you throw a huge party?!" (Luke 15:28–30, author paraphrase).

Do you see how similar the older brother is to the younger—how similar the brothers are to each other? The older brother is a hard worker. He toes the line and does what he is told. The expectation is the same as his younger brother: He should get what he earns. The older son understands his relationship to his father in the same way. While the younger son wants to earn his place through servanthood because he's done wrong, the obedient son thinks he has earned his place through all he's done right. Both sons base their relationship with their father on what they have or have not done.

They are both self-reliant. They have not yet learned what it is to be a son.

The parable ends without resolution. Will the sons learn what it means to be sons of their father? The absence of resolution invites the hearer to ask the same questions. Do I relate to God as a servant? Is my relationship based on my worth? Or is my relationship based on my identity as the father's child?

TRANSACTIONAL SPIRITUALITY

The brothers represent a common way of relating to God, a way that I will call Transactional Spirituality. Transactional Spirituality says, "If I do this, then God will. . ." Or, "If I *don't* do this, God will. . ." We see this in the life of both of the sons, and this is one way to understand *Relying on God* from the perspective of what we rely on God *for*.

A Transactional Spirituality gives the appearance of faith, but it is actually the absence of faith because it depends on us. We can find this kind of bartering with God in the scripture story, but its presence in the scripture is not an affirmation of the approach. We must be careful when we read the scripture to not affirm something simply because it is present in the scripture. Particularly as Anabaptists, we affirm what aligns with Jesus, who is the full revelation of God. That which does not align with God revealed in Christ tells us something, more often than not, about humanity and our (mis)perceptions of God. A Transactional Spirituality shows us that we, like the brothers, have not yet learned what it is to be children of God.

In my role as pastor, I pray regularly with people. I often pray for healing. Transactional Spirituality assumes that God's answer to my prayer says something about me. If God answers, then I have prayed a good prayer or have been found worthy to have an audience with God. However, most often when I pray for chronic conditions like cancer or infertility or struggles with mental health, there is no healing of the condition. Transactional Spirituality causes me to question myself and God. Did I not have enough faith, or did I not pray the right words? Is there something wrong with me or the other person that caused God to not answer this prayer?

Notice how these questions center on us and not the nature and character of God. These questions lead to a burdensome weight. Sometimes they lead to doubting our faith altogether because the formula we have been given is not working like it should. In the worst cases, Christians use a "failed transaction" as a way to shame other Christians into trying harder, as if the answer is dependent on us. Do you notice how *Relying on God* in this way is really relying on us?

Growing up in the church my whole life, and having a behind-the-scenes look as a pastor for over twenty years, I would suggest Transactional Spirituality has made the church, and its leaders, tired. No wonder there is so much burnout and so much disunity. This is what happens when the story is so small, when the story centers on us and not God. The formula is not working.

Perhaps we are more functional atheists than we want to admit.

INCARNATIONAL SPIRITUALITY

In contrast to the transactional nature of the brothers, we see in the father what we could call an Incarnational

Spirituality—meaning the coming of God to us. The father runs to one brother and embraces him in his shame, not even allowing the son to get out the words to his preplanned speech. The father leaves the party to find the elder brother, reminding him, "Everything I have is yours." Yours already. Yours based upon who you are as children because of who I AM as your father.

Invitation to covenant

The father in the story is representative of what theologian Walter Brueggeman calls "covenantal fidelity,"[3] and the story itself carries with it the idea of covenant. Covenant is a committed relationship between two parties, and throughout the Old Testament, covenant is the way Israel understands its relationship to God. God calls Israel into relationship and gives them ways to live in relationship. Like the two sons, Israel continually fails their part of the covenant, which *should* mean God ends the relationship. But God does not. God keeps fidelity to the covenant(s) not because of how Israel fulfills their responsibilities, but because this is the nature of God to do so.

Relying on God begins with God, not us. It flows from the nature of who God is. The different covenants reveal God's nature to us as God responds in fidelity to one broken covenant after another. Eventually the prophet Jeremiah introduces the idea of a new covenant, based not on Israel's ability to respond, but upon God's incarnational nature to be made known and enter into (Jeremiah 31:31–34). This covenant will be based upon the desire of God to forgive, not on Israel's ability to fulfill. The new covenant comes to Israel in the flesh in the person of Jesus. The fidelity of Jesus to God, and to God's people, is the ultimate communication of God's reliability, on which we build our lives.

Jesus has given us a means of grace to experience the reality of the new covenant in an ongoing way in the context of the church. There are few other practices within historic Christianity that communicate more to us the heart of God and our identity as God's beloved children then the practice of communion, or the Lord's Supper. Communion is both a way to understand, and a way to participate in what it means to rely on God.

Receiving communion

Several years ago, our church transitioned to receiving communion as a weekly part of our corporate worship. Prior to that our practice was typical of most BIC churches, making communion a part of our gathered worship either monthly or a few times a year. As you can imagine, it caused a bit of stir.

The most common pushback initially was this: "If we take it every week, it won't mean as much!" Just as with Transactional Spirituality, this statement centers on the self. The assumption is that I bring the meaning to the table. It only means something if I feel it does. But we do not ascribe meaning to communion; communion is meaningful because God has given it meaning. Communion ascribes meaning to us, and the meaning of communion comes from none other than Jesus himself.

As we began receiving communion weekly, people shared sad stories of how the table had been used in a transactional way. Some shared how leaders of the church would come to their home to make sure they were in a "right place" to receive communion. Another person shared how there was a separate room people would need to enter to be questioned whether they were ready to receive communion. One person was actually afraid to receive communion because of the fear induced from a previous church experience. Many had received the message that you needed to be in the right place in order to receive the body and blood of Christ. Can you notice the ways that Transactional Spirituality shapes how we come to God?

We do not clean ourselves up in order to come to the table. Such striving has no place in God's kingdom. Paul reminds us that it was "while we were *still sinners*, Christ died for us" (Romans 5:8 NIV, emphasis added). The cross has cleansed and continues to cleanse, and the grace of this sacrament invites us to experience it week after week and moment after moment.

Receiving communion each week centered our congregation on Jesus like nothing else has. At the end of the service each Sunday, the work of Jesus is proclaimed, the invitation is given, and we are invited to respond. We proclaim week after week that "Jesus has set this table (he is the host), and anyone who desires to receive the grace and mercy of Jesus are invited to receive (we are his guests)."

Relying on God means responding to what God has done and continues to do. Relying does not come from trying hard to rely. It is a posture of responsiveness to the covenantal fidelity of God expressed through the life, death, and resurrection of Jesus. Communion is a sacrament and grace given to the church to help us experience this truth. Just as we respond by coming forward to receive the bread and the cup, *Relying on God* is the ongoing act of bringing our whole life to God, not keeping anything back, and surrendering it to him.

LIVING PRAYERFULLY

Receiving communion helps us visualize and imagine what it means for us to "live prayerfully" as we *Rely on God*. Prayer is communion, and communion is prayer.

There is a gnostic thread woven through the language and practice of the church that undermines the place of prayer and communion with God. Gnosticism is the philosophical belief glorifying the spiritual and deeming the flesh and physical corrupt. Gnostic language is prevalent in the church, particularly around gathered worship and receiving communion. This language shapes how we relate to God outside of gathered worship. How many of us have heard or used the following kind of language?

> *We invite you to leave all of your distractions at the door.*
> *Leave all those things that have been weighing you down.*
> *Let them go and come worship the Lord.*

This idea is gnostic because it separates and divides the person. They are to leave the (physical) realities of their life at the door or outside the sanctuary so they can enter in and worship the Lord (spiritual). This kind of language is so common it has become acceptable and normative, but what it does is keep us from bringing our whole selves to God. This kind of thinking is transactional and has kept people from experiencing the new covenant based on the fidelity of Christ.

Instead, can we imagine an invitation to bring it all: the morning fight between spouses and screaming kids, the depression, the failures of the week, the doubts, the sin, the hopelessness? Take a moment to visualize the beauty of this, slowly walking toward the communion table, bringing all of these things with you. Imagine the invitation to come and the invitation to receive the fidelity of Christ in the midst of the burdens and brokenness you bring. Christ's broken body as daily bread. Christ's blood cleansing and renewing, pronouncing forgiveness.

This is what it means to pray. Prayer is collecting the scattered pieces of our lives and bringing them to the care of God.

Prayer is not a time to separate from the world to be with God. Prayer is the time to bring the world to God. Prayer is the space where we stop trying to figure everything out, where we cease the scheming and recognize the futility of our own efforts. Prayer is an act of surrender and an immersion into the faithfulness of God. Prayer is rest.

To the many of us who have been shaped by Transactional Spirituality, this understanding is perhaps counterintuitive, passive, or unproductive. Transactional Spirituality demands activity—ours and God's. We fill the space of prayer with requests while God responds with instruction or action. When we read the phrase "living prayerfully," our minds immediately flit to the spoken activity of prayer and the time we set aside to "present your requests to God" (Philippians 4:6 NIV). To be clear, God certainly welcomes our requests! The question is not whether or not we should make requests of God, but whether they are made transactionally or relying on God's covenantal fidelity.

Postures of prayer

There are three postures of prayer that lead us in becoming a people who rely on God: receiving, resting, and returning. We use the word *posture* instead of *practice* because posture is a more imaginative word. Posture helps us visualize how we go about doing things, whereas practice focuses on what it is we are doing. Perhaps we could say these postures help us visualize what it looks like as we rely on God.

Receiving. Relying on God is a response to God. As such, God offers us something, and we receive it. We receive it not because we earned it, but because God is offering it. Receiving is a posture of open hands where all is received as gift and grace. God desires to give good gifts to his children, and part of *Relying on God* is learning to receive those gifts as God's children.

Continually we learn how to receive. As we continue to follow Jesus, we grow in understanding what it means to be God's child. The grounding of our identity deepens in God's love for us. Each act of mercy God has shown us deepens our reliance on him. But are we not still confronted with how frequently we relate to God transactionally? We then return to communion with God and receive. The bread pressed into our palms. The cup of juice given to us. "This is my body, broken for you. This is my blood, shed for you" (see 1 Corinthians 11:24). We are reminded again of God's desire for us to receive this—to receive his life once again.

The open hands that receive the bread and cup become the posture of our hands and heart in prayer. In this case, the open hands are representative of receiving God into what is in our lives. Our prayers move beyond asking God to get us out of whatever it is we face. Instead, we open our hands and receive Christ into what is happening. We ask and imagine how Jesus is entering into our lives. The circumstances we want to avoid become a place of communion with God.

Resting. The posture of receiving leads us to a place of rest. *Relying on God* is resting in God.

This is not how we enter prayer, but this is what we find in prayer. More often than not we are driven to prayer by anxiety or the feelings of being overwhelmed. All the "fors" are front and center. The functionally atheist part of our heart causes us to conjure up solutions that are within our control of implementing. Their success or failure is up to us. It is all too much.

With open hands, we hold these things before God, receiving God into them. As we do, we find rest. This rest is marked by quiet. Over the years, our identity becomes more deeply rooted in God, as God's child. Our places of prayer enter new rooms in times of silence. We will cease needing to speak, so much as simply being still and knowing that God is God (Psalm 46:10).

Silence is not lack of presence, but fuller presence. It comes from a place of rest, of trusting, as Julian of Norwich has said, that "all is well and all manner of things shall be well."[4] Is all well in the world? No. Is God, God? Yes. Then all is well and we can rest.

This is a sabbath way of life with God. "Living prayerfully" is living from a place of rest, where our souls have found rest in God alone (Psalm 62:5 author paraphrase). We enter into prayer to find rest, and we leave prayer to engage the world from a place of rest. *Relying on God* through prayer allows us to enter and engage the world with a nonanxious presence. We "will not fear, though the earth give way" as we have made "the God of Jacob is our fortress" (Psalm 46:2, 11, NIV).

Relying on God and rest cannot be separated. The more we are anxious about all that needs to be done, even that which we feel has to be done for the kingdom and for God, the more it reveals that we are at the center.

Returning. It is a beautiful thing to grow in reliance upon the Lord. Hopefully we all have experienced wonderful seasons of learning how to receive and rest in God. But do we not also experience how quickly and easily our hearts twist them into a false sense of security leading to a faith, a way of living, or a form of leadership centered on ourselves? The open hands that received from God, over time, become closed. What was a gift has become a right. What was freely given has become a possession and something that is ours to control.

We must return even the good things over to God, again and again, lest they take the place of God. We must surrender even God's good gifts back to God. It is a question we can all ask ourselves: What good gifts in my life do I need to surrender so they do not take the place of God?

When we rely on God for something, and God answers, we will always come to the place where we must reckon with God's answer becoming an idol. We can become so connected to God as we seek God for something that when the something is given, it takes the place of God. It becomes an idol and ultimately a source of disappointment and frustration because what was being sought was not God, but seeking God for something else.

We will always face the temptation to let what God gives take the place of who God is. Too quickly we become reliant upon the gift and not the Giver. This may be why so many of us get stuck in the past with our faith formation. We think God is not present now because God is not showing up how God did in the past. We are tempted to think that God has moved on. It is fine to build an altar in remembrance of beautiful places with God, but we must also be aware that altars turn into places of idolatry.

The communion table invites us to return again and again, to remember. God is not surprised by our once-open hands becoming closed. God knows this will happen and invites us to open them again. After particularly hard weeks where our open hands have turned into clenched fists, we are invited to open them again to receive the body of Christ, broken for us.

CONCLUSION

What we rely on God for will differ from person to person and context to context, but this is not the basis of *Relying on God*. The God who sets a table for us in Thailand is the same God that sets it for us in Zimbabwe and Canada. It is the same

God who established a covenant of fidelity with Israel in the wilderness, and with the church through Christ. It is this God who meets our brother in Nicaragua and our sister in India as they gather the scattered pieces of their lives and bring them to a place of prayer. In that place of prayer, a child in Guatemala and an elderly woman in Spain receive the incarnational presence of Christ and find a shared rest that comes from relying on God. We all come from different places, but we're all learning to rely on the same God.

· · · · · · · · · · · · · · · · ·

RESPONSE ESSAY

Relying on God

▶ *Stephen Badiger, Goa, India*

"We have no power. . . we do not know what to do. . . but our eyes *are* on you," (2 Chronicles 20:12 NIV, emphasis added), was the cry of King Jehoshapat as he faced the looming threat of a vast army prepared to attack the people of God. Jehoshaphat and his people sought the Lord's assistance. Frequently, in our daily lives, as we commit to following Christ, we encounter situations that render us feeling powerless and often bewildered. We resonate with King Jehoshaphat as we acknowledge our own lack of power and understanding. Regrettably, we often fail to fully fix our gaze upon God and instead lean on our own strengths, knowledge, and resources.

As followers of Christ, we are extended an invitation to rely on God in every situation of our lives, just as we see in the story of King Jehoshaphat, where God reassured the King, saying, "Do not be afraid. . . For the battle is not yours, but God's" (2 Chronicles 20:15 NIV). While many of us intellectually grasp the concept of *Relying on God*, it often proves challenging to live this out in our daily lives. Frequently, the hurdles are entwined with cultural influences and our transactional tendency to barter with God. Nevertheless, God's lavish love, unending grace, and ceaseless mercies persistently teach and draw us toward his truth, enabling us to turn to him in every moment of our lives.

THE LURE OF TRANSACTIONAL SPIRITUALITY

In India, where more than 330 million deities are worshiped with billions of rituals and traditions to please gods and goddesses, more often than not, Christians become a victim of Transactional Spirituality. People who are accustomed to performing rituals to keep their gods happy to receive blessings struggle with *Relying on God* and often resort to modern-day pharisaism to feel that they have earned the blessings. Though we teach about relying on God for everything in the church, in reality, most of the time, most would rely on their own strength and resources, relying on God only for the things that seem out of their reach.

Our churches in West India, where most of the people come from Hindu backgrounds, find it very difficult to accept the free gift of salvation and to rely on God for everything, including every breath that we take.

AN INVITATION TO RELY

When the global pandemic hit the church, it affected every individual with regards to health, economic stability, or emotional well-being.

Our church in Goa, India, faced several challenges during the global pandemic that led us to fully rely on God. The dire need of basic necessities such as food and shelter and our inability to meet them was an invitation to rely on God.

Amidst economic struggles tied to seasonal employment in Goa's tourist industry, the church's migrant members faced dire living conditions, lacking necessities and medical supplies. Technologically, the shift to virtual worship was hindered by limited internet access and digital literacy. Meanwhile, confronting widespread misinformation and conspiracy theories proved to be a scientific challenge for the church's less-educated congregations.

During those times when we were learning the needs of the people, physical and spiritual, on a daily basis, we realized and acknowledged our inability to meet those needs. In that most critical time God taught the church what *Relying on God* would mean.

The crisis necessitated a shift in our perspective. Sermons needed to address pressing concerns such as the importance of connecting science and spirituality, obeying authorities, and embracing new ways of worship. In the backdrop of India's diverse spiritual landscape, the pandemic served as a catalyst for a transformative spiritual experience. The intricate tapestry of rituals, once seen as the measure of one's faith, was challenged. The pandemic underscored that *Relying on God* is not about adhering to external rituals in a transactional relationship where we assume that God would bless us only if we go to church, but rather, it is about embracing a living relationship marked by trust and surrender.

OUR RESPONSE TO GOD

In those trying times God taught us that *Relying on God* meant:

Turning to him: Our first-ever meditation and encouragement shared through the WhatsApp message was taken from the book of Psalms 121:1–2, "I lift up my eyes to the mountains, where does my help come from? My help comes from the LORD, the Maker of heaven and earth" (NIV). We acknowledged that despite globalization, advanced medical technologies, and transportation, nothing would come to our aid except the Lord himself. We would rely on him to provide our daily bread not just in terms of an expression, but in reality.

Waiting on him: We learned to fully rely on God to meet all of our physical and spiritual needs. Part of *Relying on God* meant to wait on the Lord for his deliverance. While we continued to rely on God in waiting, God opened doors through the Global Compassion Fund and through the sacrificial offerings of fellow BIC members and friends across the United States and Canada. Through these gifts we started sending care packages that included food supplies to needy families. This outreach extended not only to our church believers but also to their neighbors who were struggling for each meal.

Returning to the truth: We often meditated and reminded ourselves of the passages where God teaches us to obey human authorities appointed by God (Romans 13:1–7; 1 Peter 2:13–14). We learned that *Relying on God* meant obeying God's Word by respecting government guidelines such as social distancing, masking, and later vaccination. We encouraged each other to stay away from fake news and rumors. Amid the pandemic, we adopted audio conference calls for daily prayers, expanding worship beyond physical church space. Embracing masks and social distancing showcased our trust in God's wisdom and faith in divine providence during uncertain times.

RESTING AND RETURNING TO GOD

Amidst these trials, the church embraced its foundational calling to be a beacon of hope. It was a reminder that the essence of *Relying on God* is not confined to grand gestures but thrives in the simplicity of daily acts of love and support. We realized that the key to *Relying on God* lies in recognizing our role as his children and resting in the assurance that he is in control.

One of the most critical and once-in-a-generation pandemics taught us how our physical strength, our network of people or resources, can mean nothing in the blink of an eye, but trusting God and relying on him can open doors even in the most hopeless moments.

The pandemic era has shown us that true reliance on God is not a one-time decision but an ongoing posture of the heart.

Just as the early disciples waited for the Holy Spirit's guidance (Acts 1:4), we too must adopt a posture of waiting, trusting and returning to God's presence.

· · · · · · · · · · · · · · · · · ·
RESPONSE ESSAY
Relying on God

▶ *Kerry Hoke, Harrisburg, Pennsylvania*

When we are young and strong and filled with dreams for the future, a future that lies in the vastness before us, we all too easily succumb to the siren song of self-reliance. But as we journey through life and experience its blows and stings, do we know whose we are? As we age and experience the loss of who we once were and what we once could do, do we scramble to find some way to cope, to pull ourselves out of the spin? Or do we have a well-worn resting place in our Father God that fills us with a peaceful confidence that *all is well and all manner of things shall be well*?

Our American culture reveres those who pull themselves up by their proverbial bootstraps with dogged determination. These stories are part of the American lore—the revolutionaries, the pioneers of western expansion—and the foundations of the American republic—capitalism, those "inalienable rights" of life, liberty, and the pursuit of happiness. Conversely, *Relying on God* demands a kind of dependence to which we Americans are especially not accustomed. It requires a recognition and acceptance of our limitations and brokenness. Both are antithetical to the individualistic and self-made air we breathe and water we drink.

For the last six years, I have worked at Messiah Lifeways, a retirement community in Mechanicsburg, Pennsylvania. I have been surrounded by people who, because of their age, find themselves experiencing an array of physical limitations and acutely aware of an increasing loss of the energy, strength, and vigor of their younger years. Some live in denial. Some rebel against it. But they're all grappling with losses, losses that require them to be dependent in ways they haven't before—on people, on medicine, on assistive devices, and on God.

A rare few possess and exhibit a deep peace. They are the ones who have come to terms with their frail and failing forms, and it is well with their souls. These are my muses, the ones in whose footsteps I long to follow—undaunted by their limitations because they know God intimately and have learned to rely on him. They have tasted his goodness; they have lived under his faithful hand; they have been shaped and molded by his abundant love. Through the years, they have cultivated a reliance on God that compels them to respond to who God is and what God is doing no matter the circumstance. For them, reliance on God long ago became a way of life, a daily commitment to die to self in pursuit of the one who says, "Follow me!" (Matthew 4:19).

The apostle Paul put it this way: "Outwardly we are wasting away, yet inwardly we are being renewed day by day" (2 Corinthians 4:16 NIV). This kind of inner renewal is not automatic or passive. Real and lasting renewal comes from an intentional and deliberate reliance on God that is cultivated through prayer and communion with God's Spirit in the deepest part of our souls. By adopting a "posture of responsiveness to the covenantal fidelity of God," we begin to realize and respond to the ongoing pursuit of God towards us.

DETACHED RELIANCE

At first, though I found it easy to minister to the older adults at Messiah Lifeways with compassion and gentleness, I also did so in a detached sort of way. I could walk alongside them in their limitations and "wasting away," but I was asleep to my own limitations. I was operating with an unexamined conviction that my own youthful energy and able-bodiedness provided me with everything I needed to do the work I was called to do. I was relying far more on the pride of my own abilities than from an openhanded reception of God's good gifts to me.

One memorable fall down the stairs in my home in March 2021 woke me up. As I lay in the hospital bed with my broken ankle temporarily set and splinted, the orthopedic surgeon came into the room to explain the surgery I would undergo the next day and the road to recovery that would follow. Three plates and twelve pins would bind my ankle together, and I would spend the better part of three months not walking. My bones needed the time to heal, to calcify, to be knit back together, and putting any weight at all on my left side would jeopardize that healing.

Throughout those three months, I received an excruciating lesson in humility, limitations, and dependence. I had no choice but to rely on my husband to help me with the most basic of tasks. I relied on family and dear friends for meals and companionship as I was bound to the couch for the first several weeks.

EMBRACING INCARNATIONAL SPIRITUALITY

Is it not at our point of need that God meets us? Truthfully, we are always in need. The power comes when we awaken to our helplessness and willingly rely on God to be our all in all. The transformation comes when we joyfully surrender to our loving Creator, who then spreads out a lavish banquet for us as sons and daughters, revealing to us with disarming intimacy his high and wide and deep and long amazing love for us.

I relied on God in prayer, sometimes with the most desperate cries for mercy, and in the stillness of the forced cessation of activity, he met me. In my moment of need, he lovingly embraced me and revealed his faithfulness to me in new ways.

Even now, I find myself entering an unknown season with opportunity to rely on God in new ways. I leave behind a job with stability and predictability in order to follow God's call to bring what he has given me to meet the brokenness of the world with his light and love. It's testing my trust once again. As long as I've walked with God, I still wrestle with the ego that wants to be in control, to know what's around the corner, to pull up the proverbial bootstraps. But I know as I choose over and over again to rely on God, he is refining me more and more into the likeness of Christ in the process.

And that is my ultimate desire as a follower of Jesus, as it is for all of us.

. . . .
CHAPTER 10

Discussion Questions

1. Why are we tempted by Transactional Spirituality? Within this framework why are we inclined to define our relationship with God in an *if-then* way? What dangers are present when we "barter with God" when *Relying on God*?

2. Read the following poem by Jewish mystic Levi Yitzchak:

   > *Where I wander — You!*
   > *Where I ponder — You!*
   > *Only You, You again, always You!*
   > *You! You! You!*
   > *When I am gladdened — You!*
   > *When I am saddened — You!*
   > *Only You, You again, always You!*
   > *You! You! You!*
   > *Sky is You! Earth is You!*
   > *You above! You below!*
   > *In every trend, at every end,*
   > *Only You, You again, always You!*
   > *You! You! You!*[5]

   If we approach the God-human relationship in the way the poem suggests, what does it say about our identity as children of God? How can the poem help move us toward an Incarnational Spirituality?

3. In what way(s) can we bring our whole selves to prayer and communion? Why is it critical that we shed our dualistic tendencies when *Relying on God*?

4. In living prayerfully, compare a *doing* vs. *being* approach to prayer. Why does the writer link *doing* to Transactional Spirituality?

5. Read Luke 15:11–32. Consider way(s) you tend to be self-reliant. How do you relate as a servant and a child of God, as illustrated in the parable?

For Further Reading

CHAPTER 1

Bunyan, John. *Grace Abounding to the Chief of Sinners.* Abbotsford, WI: Aneko Press, 2018.

Manning, Brennan. *The Ragamuffin Gospel.* Colorado Springs, CO: Multnomah, 2005.

Wittlinger, Carlton O. *Quest for Piety and Obedience. The Story of the Brethren in Christ.* Nappanee, IN: Evangel Press, 1978.

Wright, N. T. *Surprised by Hope.* New York: HarperOne, 2018.

CHAPTER 2

Good, Meghan. *The Bible Unwrapped: Making Sense of Scripture Today.* Harrisonburg, VA: Herald Press, 2018.

Keen, Karen. *The Word of a Humble God: The Origins, Inspiration, and Interpretation of Scripture.* Grand Rapids, MI: Eerdmans, 2022.

McKnight, Scot. *The Blue Parakeet: Rethinking How You Read the Bible.* Grand Rapids, MI: Zondervan, 2008.

Richards, Randolph, and B.J. O'Brien. *Misreading Scripture with Western Eyes: Removing Cultural Blinders to Better Understand the Bible.* Downers Grove, IL: InterVarsity Press, 2012.

Roth, Frederico. *Reading the Bible Around the World: A Student's Guide to Global Hermeneutics*. Downers Grove, IL: InterVarsity Press, 2022.

CHAPTER 3

Brethren in Christ History and Life, vol. 23, no. 1, April 2000.

Cherry, Constance. *The Worship Architect: A Blueprint for Designing Culturally Relevant and Biblically Faithful Services*. Grand Rapids, MI: Baker, 2010.

Smith, James K.A. *You Are What You Love: The Spiritual Power of Habit*. Grand Rapids, MI: Brazos Press, 2016.

CHAPTER 4

Bonhoeffer, Dietrich. *The Cost of Discipleship*. New York: Pocket Books, 1995.

Gonzalez, Antonio. *God's Reign and the End of Empires*. Miami: Convivium Press, 2012.

Peterson, Eugene. *A Long Obedience in the Same Direction*. Downers Grove, IL: InterVarsity Press, 2021.

CHAPTER 5

Baker, Mark D. *Centered-Set Church: Discipleship and Community Without Judgmentalism*. Downers Grove, IL: InterVarsity Press, 2021.

Bonhoeffer, Dietrich. *Life Together*. Minneapolis, MN: Fortress Press, 2015.

Crabb, Larry. *The Safest Place on Earth*. Nashville, TN: Word Publishing Group, 1999.

Crouch, Andy. *The Life We're Looking For: Reclaiming Relationship in a Technological World*. New York: Convergent Books, 2022.

Henricks, Michel, and Jim Wilder. *The Other Half of Church: Christian Community, Brain Science, and Overcoming Spiritual Stagnation*. Chicago: Moody Publishers, 2020.

Wilder, Jim. *Renovated: God, Dallas Willard, and the Church That Transforms*. Colorado Springs, CO: NavPress, 2020.

CHAPTER 6

Elmer, Duane. *Cross-Cultural Servanthood*. Downers Grove, IL: InterVarsity Press, 2006.

Katongole, Emmanuel M., Jonathan Wilson-Hartgrove, et al. *A Mirror to the Church: Resurrecting Faith After Genocide in Rwanda*. New York: Harper Christian, 2009.

Robertson, Dwight. *You are God's Plan A, There is no Plan B*. Colorado Springs, CO: David C Cook, 2010.

CHAPTER 7

James, Larry M. *The Wealth of the Poor: How Valuing Every Neighbor Restores Hope in Our Cities*. Abilene, Texas: Abilene Christian University Press, 2013.

McKnight, Scot, and Laura Barringer. *A Church Called Tov: Forming a Goodness Culture*. Carol Stream, IL: Tyndale House Publishers, 2020.

Sider, Ronald J. *Living Like Jesus: Eleven Essentials for Growing a Genuine Faith*. Grand Rapids, MI: Baker Books, 1996.

Thurman, Howard. *Jesus and the Disinherited*. Boston, MA: Beacon Press, 1976.

Winner, Lauren F. *Wearing God*. New York: HarperCollins Publishers, 2015.

CHAPTER 8

Brown, Dale. W. *Biblical Pacifism*. Nappanee, IN: Brethren Press, 2003.

Klaassen, Walter. *Anabaptism in Outline: Selected Primary Sources*. Kitchener, ON: Herald Press, 1981.

Kraybill, Donald B. *The Upside–Down Kingdom*. Harrisonburg, VA: Herald Press, 2011.

Murray, Stuart. *The Naked Anabaptist. The Bare Essentials of a Radical Faith*. Harrisonburg, VA: Herald Press, 2015.

Sider, E. Morris, and Luke Keefer Jr. *A Peace Reader*. Nappanee, IN: Evangel Publishing House, 2002.

CHAPTER 9

Sider, Ronald J. *Rich Christians in an Age of Hunger: Moving from Affluence to Generosity*. 6th ed., Nashville, TN: Thomas Nelson, 2015.

Staton, Tyler. *Praying Like Monks, Living Like Fools: An Invitation to the Wonder and Mystery of Prayer*. Grand Rapids, MI: Zondervan, 2022.

CHAPTER 10

Book of Common Prayer. Legare Street Press, 2023.

Brown Taylor, Barbara. *An Altar in the World*. New York: HarperOne, 2010.

Chittister, Joan. *Wisdom Distilled from the Daily*. San Francisco: Harper, 1991.

Nouwen, Henri. *The Way of the Heart*. New York: Harper Collins, 2016.

Williams, Rowan. *Being Christian: Baptism, Bible, Eucharist, Prayer*. London: SPCK Publishing, 2014.

Notes

INTRODUCTION

1. See Pia Silva, "Core Values: What They Are, Why They Matter and How They can Transform Your Business," *Forbes*, October 12, 2021, https://www.forbes.com/sites/piasilva/2021/10/12/core-values-what-they-are-why-they-matter-and-how-they-can-transform-your-business/.

2. See Nate Dvorak and Bailey Nelson, "Few Employees Believe in Their Company's Values," Gallup, September 13, 2016, https://news.gallup.com/businessjournal/195491/few-employees-believe-company-values.aspx.

3. See Ron Carucci, "How Corporate Values Get Hijacked and Misused," *Harvard Business Review*, May 29, 2017, https://hbr.org/2017/05/how-corporate-values-get-hijacked-and-misused.

4. Abraham Joshua Heschel, *Man's Quest for God* (Sante Fe, NM: Aurora Press, 1998), 93.

CHAPTER 1

1. Juan de Valdés, *Comentario a los salmos* (Madrid, Librería Nacional y Extranjera, 1885). Reimpreso en Editorial Clie, Terrasa, 1987, Salmo X, 58.

2. "Confession of Faith of the Brethren," in Carleton O. Wittlinger, *Quest for Piety and Obedience: The Story of the Brethren in Christ* (Nappanee, IN: Evangel Press, 1978), 551.

3. Dietrich Bonhoeffer, *Cost of Discipleship* (New York: Macmillan, 1959), 37.

CHAPTER 2

1. You can read about the meeting in A. Brubaker et al., "A Review of The Study Conference on a Brethren in Christ Interpretation of Scripture," *Brethren in Christ History and Life* 9 (1986): 276–283. For more on why the BIC has not used inerrancy, see Luke Keefer, "'Innerancy' and the Brethren in Christ," *Brethren in Christ History and Life* 15 (1992): 3–17.

2. *Battle for the Bible* is the title of the book by Harold Lindsell (Grand Rapids, MI: Zondervan, 1976), who wrote in the midst of this conversation. The origin of the

debate goes back to the late 1800s, but the BIC seem to be mostly unaware of it until the BIC begin engaging theological discussions outside their close-knit communities in the mid-twentieth century. See L. M. Yoder, "Why Have We Changed the Way We Interpret the Bible?," in *The Brethren in Christ and Biblical Interpretation: A Series of Study Papers Sponsored by Renewal 2000 Phase II Task Force* (Nappanee, IN: Evangel Press, 1990), pages 14–21.

3. Keefer, "Inerrancy," 12–13.

4. Brubaker et al., "A Review," 281.

5. The BIC believe translations of the Bible are also God's Word. The BIC believe that all the words of the Bible are inspired by God. Historically, the BIC have accepted diverse views regarding the nature of inspiration and have resisted modern frameworks like inerrancy, infallibility, etc.

6. For those who do not find my conclusion convincing, I give permission to ignore the attribution to Adam, but not the most important thing, that misplaced fear as a motivation to reject God's words out of fear is present in the expanded command, whether one attributes it to Adam, Eve, or an unknown source.

7. "Articles of Faith and Doctrine, Article I," in *Manual of Doctrine and Government* (Mechanicsburg, PA: Brethren in Christ U.S., 2022), 5.

8. "What We Believe about the Bible." https://bicus.org/wp-content/uploads/2017/05/Statement-Scripture.pdf.

9. For this and more insights on these ideas, see Daryl Climenhaga, "Interpreting the Scriptures," *Brethren in Christ History and Life* 10 (1987): 198–209.

10. Climenhaga, 204.

CHAPTER 3

1. James K. A. Smith, *You Are What You Love: The Spiritual Power of Habit* (Grand Rapids, MI: Brazos Press, 2016), 22.

2. David Foster Wallace, in Smith, 23.

3. Wallace, in Smith, 23.

4. Terry L. Brensinger, "A Brethren in Christ Theology of Worship" in *Brethren in Christ History and Life*, 23, no. 1 (April 2000): 129.

5. Smith, *You Are What You Love*, 25.

6. Smith, 24.

7. Brensinger, "A Brethren in Christ Theology," 129–131, offers this helpful three-part framework as the basis for worship throughout history.

8. Brensinger, 128.

9. Calvin Institute of Christian Worship, "Four-Fold Pattern of Worship," September 17, 2014, https://worship.calvin.edu/resources/resource-library/four-fold-pattern-of-worship/#.

10. Since the last half of the nineteenth century, the BIC have compiled and used music resources in hymn format. The most recent is *Hymns for Praise and Worship* (Nappanee, IN: Evangel Publishing House, 1984).

11. The teaching and mentoring of Dr. Dwight Thomas contribute to this section.

12. For more, see Kara Powell, Jake Mulder and Brad Griffin, *Growing Young: Six Essential Strategies to Help Young People Discover and Love Your Church* (Grand Rapids, MI: Baker Books, 2016); and Kara Powell and Chap Clark, *Sticky Faith: Everyday Ideas to Build Lasting Faith in Your Kids* (Grand Rapids, MI: Zondervan, 2011).

13. Credit is due to Dr. Doug Curry, worship pastor at Messiah University, for calling attention to these important dynamics.

14. "Articles of Faith and Doctrine," in *Manual of Doctrine and Government* (Mechanicsburg, PA: Brethren in Christ U.S., 2022).

15. "Articles of Faith and Doctrine."

16. Brensinger, "A Brethren in Christ Theology," 141.

17. Brett McCracken, "21 Challenges Facing the 21st Century Church," October 27, 2016, https://www.brettmccracken.com/blog/blog/2016/10/27/21-challenges-facing-the-21st-century-church/.

18. Chris Stoke-Walker, "How Smartphones and Social Media Are Changing Christianity," February 22, 2017, https://www.bbc.com/future/article/20170222-how-smartphones-and-social-media-are-changing-religion.

19. Stephen Victor Coertze, "Challenges Facing the African Church: South African Theologians Speak Out" (MA diss., University of Pretoria, 2005), https://repository.up.ac.za/bitstream/handle/2263/28004/dissertation.pdf;sequence=1.

20. Chelsea Rollman, "The Estranged Church: National Missionaries Train Prosperity Gospel Pastors in Zimbabwe," June 6, 2023, https://www.mtw.org/stories/details/the-estranged-church-national-missionaries-train-prosperity-gospel-pastors-in-zimbabwe.

21. Vhumani Magezi and Peter Manzanga, "Prosperity and Health Ministry as a Coping Mechanism in the Poverty and Suffering Context of Zimbabwe: A Pastoral Evaluation and Response," SciELO, 2016, http://www.scielo.org.za/scielo.php?script=sci_arttext&pid=S2305-08532016000100018.

22. Thinandavha D. Mashau and Mookgo S. Kgatle, "Prosperity Gospel and the Culture of Greed in Post-Colonial Africa: Constructing an Alternative African Christian Theology of Ubuntu," SciELO, 2019, http://www.scielo.org.za/scielo.php?script=sci_arttext&pid=S2074-77052019000100009.

CHAPTER 4

1. "Core Values," Brethren in Christ U.S., last modified April 13, 2018, https://bicus.org/about/what-we-believe/core-values/.

2. Anabaptism at 500 staff, *Reading Scripture Together: Participant Guide* (Harrisonburg, VA: MennoMedia, 2022), https://anabaptismat500.com/wp-content/uploads/2023/02/A500-Bible-Study-Guide-participant2.pdf.

3. UNFPA Zimbabwe, *Inter-Censal Demographic Survey, 2017* (Harare: Zimbabwe National Statistics Agency, 2017), ix, https://zimbabwe.unfpa.org/sites/default/files/pub-pdf/Inter Censal Demography Survey 2017 Report.pdf/.

4. African proverb.

5. Tendai Ruben Mbofana, "Zimbabwe Churches Turn Evil, Please Jesus Come Back!" *The Zimbabwean*, June 5, 2023, https://www.thezimbabwean.co/2023/06/zimbabwe-churches-turn-evil-please-jesus-come-back/.

6. Emmanuel Katongole, *Mirror to the Church: Resurrecting Faith after Genocide in Rwanda* (Grand Rapids, MI: Zondervan, 2009).

7. This is a common song in southern Africa. No known historiographic material is available to explain its origins. Excitement in the song can be heightened by clapping and tapping. Often one stanza of the song is sung. Choristers can innovate what they include in other stanzas. Though the song has existed in oral and aural community memory, recent hymnody has included it in the Mennonite hymnal called *Voices Together* (Harrisonburg, VA: MennoMedia, 2020).

8. I have purposely included the Mennonite World Conference as a global commune and far-reaching fraternity in local and global witness, where the Brethren in Christ Church holds membership.

9. Ronald J. Sider, "God's People Reconciling," 1984, at https://cpt.org/sider.

10. Cf. Luke 1:46–55.

11. Ndlovu also captures this point as he briefly exegetes Jesus' sermon in Matthew 25:31–46.

12. Cf. Matthew 6:10.

CHAPTER 5

1. Cochren & Co., "Church (Take Me Back)," Bryan Fowler, Micah Kuiper, and Michael Cochren, 2018, Essential Music Publishing LLC.

2. Jim Davis, interview with Michael Graham and Ryan Burge, Gospel Coalition, podcast audio, May 10, 2023, https://www.thegospelcoalition.org/podcasts/as-in-heaven/dechurched-america-why-leave/.

3. "Core Values," Brethren in Christ U.S., last modified April 13, 2018, https://bicus.org/about/what-we-believe/core-values/.

4. The late Dallas Willard identified a situation plaguing evangelicalism that is similar to what is troubling the BIC. See his books *The Great Omission* and *Renovated*.

5. John Stackhouse, *Evangelical Ecclesiology: Reality or Illusion* (Grand Rapids: Baker Academic, 2003), 9.

6. Harold Bender, *The Anabaptist Vision* (Waterford, Ireland: CrossReach Publications, 2017), 19.

7. Walter Klassen, *Anabaptism: Neither Catholic nor Protestant* (Waterloo, ON: Pandora Press, 2001), 24.

8. Evidence for this is found in the larger context of Hebrews 10 as well as many other passages.

9. I first encountered this idea in 2006 in Simon Chan's book *Liturgical Theology*. Since that time, I have read a similar and earlier proposal from Mennonite scholar John Driver, in his book *Understanding the Atonement for the Mission of the Church*, which was first published in 1986. In some ways the timing is irrelevant in that neither Chan nor Driver claim the perspective started with him. In fact, both understand this to be part of the church's self-understanding during its first generations.

10. Sally Lloyd-Jones, *Jesus Storybook Bible* (Grand Rapids: Zonderkidz, 2007), 36.

11. Jim Wilder and Michel Hendricks, *The Other Half of Church* (Chicago: Moody Publishers, 2020), 87.

12. Wilder and Hendricks, 95.

13. "Connect Generations," ReFocus Ministry, October 17, 2023, https://refocusministry.org/connect-generations/.

14. William Mauricio Beltrán and Sonia Larotta, *Diversidad religiosa, valores y participación política en Colombia. Resultados de la encuesta nacional sobre diversidad religiosa* (Bogotá: Universidad Nacional de Colombia, 2020).

15. Comisión Económica para América Latina y el Caribe (CEPAL), *Panorama Social de America Latina* (Santiago: Naciones Unidas, 2019).

16. "Fe y espiritualidad: herramientas para resistir y superar el conflicto armado en Colombia" in *Hacia una ética de participación y esperanza : Congreso Latinoamericano de Ética Teológica*, ed. Emilce Cuda (Bogotá: Pontificia Universidad Javeriana, 2017), 267–275.

17. Janine Abbring, "Interview with Yuval Harari," VPRO Documentary, February 19, 2022, YouTube video, 1:10:07, https://www.youtube.com/watch?v=ScJf3jWIGUE. Interestingly, the atheist Israeli academic says something very similar to what the twentieth century British Christian writer, C.S. Lewis, originally said in 1943:

    The more I resist Him and try to live on my own, the more I become dominated by my own heredity and upbringing and surroundings and natural desires. In fact what I so proudly call "Myself" becomes merely the meeting place for trains of events which I never started and which I cannot stop. What I call "My wishes" become merely the desires thrown up by my physical organism or pumped into me by other men's thoughts or even suggested to me by devils.

    Eggs and alcohol and a good night's sleep will be the real origins of what I flatter myself by regarding as my own highly personal and discriminating decision to make love to the girl opposite to me in the railway carriage. Propaganda will be the real origin of what I regard as my own personal political ideals. I am not, in my natural state, nearly so much of a person as I like to believe: most of what I call 'me' can be very easily explained. It is when I turn to Christ, when I give myself up to His Personality, that I first begin to have a real personality of my own.

    Mere Christianity (New York: Touchstone, 1996), 190.

18. Irenaeus, *Against Heresies*, Philip Schaff, trans. (Moscow, ID: Romans Road Media, 2015), 98.

19. Aristotle, *Nicomachean Ethics*, Terence Irwin, trans. (Indianapolis: Hackett Publishing, 1999), 18.

20. Charles Taylor, *Modern Social Imaginaries* (Durham: Duke University Press, 2004), 23.

CHAPTER 6

1. "Core Values," Brethren in Christ U.S., last modified April 13, 2018, https://bicus.org/about/what-we-believe/core-values/.

2. E. Morris Sider, *Stories and Scenes from a Brethren in Christ Heritage* (United States: Brethren in Christ Historical Society, 2018), 122.

3. Carlton O. Wittlinger, "Who are the Brethren in Christ? An Interpretive Essay," in *Reflections on a Heritage,* ed. E. Morris Sider (United States: Brethren in Christ Historical Society, 1999), 22.

4. Paul Boyer, *Mission on Taylor Street: The Founding and Early Years of the Dayton Brethren in Christ Mission* (Nappanee, IN: Evangel Press, 1987), 46.

5. John E Zercher, "The Brethren in Christ Accent," in *Reflections on a Heritage,* ed. E. Morris Sider (United States: Brethren in Christ Historical Society, 1999), 15.

6. Boyer, *Mission on Taylor Street*, 96–98.

7. Barbara Nkala, ed., *Celebrating the Vision: A Century of Sowing and Reaping* (Bulawayo, Zimbabwe: Brethren in Christ Church, 1998), 5.

8. "Seeking God's Glory Among All Peoples," Joshua Project, accessed April 30, 2024, https://joshuaproject.net/.

9. Due to Bijoy Roul's ongoing health challenges at the time of publication, preventing him from fully engaging with this project, the editorial team has made extensive use of his prior work in order to best capture Bijoy's voice as a respondent writer and tell the story of BIC in India in this book. Fred Holland and Bijoy Roul, *God Wants His Church to Grow* (Nappanee, IN: Evangel Press, n.d.).

CHAPTER 7

1. "Core Values," Brethren in Christ U.S., last modified April 13, 2018, https://bicus.org/about/what-we-believe/core-values/.

2. Paul Hostetler, *Brethren in Christ History and Life* 34, no. 2 (August 2011): 195–212.

3. Miroslav Volf, Matthew Croasmun, and Ryan McAnnally-Linz, *Life Worth Living: A Guide to What Matters Most* (Penguin Random House, 2023), 233.

4. Volf, Croasmun, and McAnnally-Linz, 274.

5. William Barclay, *New Testament Words* (Philadelphia, PA: Westminster Press, 1974), 11.

6. Barclay, 11–12.

7. Michael Card, *Inexpressible: Hesed and the Mystery of God's Lovingkindness* (Downer's Grove, IL: InterVarsity Press, 2018), 1–2.

8. Barclay, *New Testament Words*, 276.

9. Barclay, 277.

10. Barclay, 278.

11. Barclay, 278.

12. Barclay, 280.

13. Philip Yancey, *A Companion in Crisis: A Modern Paraphrase of John Donne's Devotions* (Littleton, CO: Illumify Media Global, 2021), 146–147.

14. Yancey, 147.

15. Shane Claiborne and Chris Haw, *Jesus for President* (Grand Rapids, MI: Zondervan, 2008), 232.

16. Nonna Verna Harrison, *God's Many-Splendored Image* (Grand Rapids, MI: Baker, 2010), 100–101.

17. Gary B. Ferngren, *Medicine and Health Care in Early Christianity* (Baltimore, MD: Johns Hopkins University Press, 2009), 129, 203.

18. Carlton O. Wittlinger, *Quest for Piety and Obedience* (Nappanee, IN: Evangel Press, 1978), 134, 177.

19. Devin Manzullo-Thomas, "Heeding God's Call," *In Part* 128, no. 3 (Fall/Winter 2015): 4, https://bicus.org/wp-content/uploads/2021/05/inpart-2015-fall-winter.pdf.

20. *Evangelical Visitor* 3, no. 4 (February 15, 1895): 12, http://bicarchives.messiah.edu/files/Documents2/1895-02-15_feb_15,1895.pdf.

21. Wittlinger, *Quest for Piety and Obedience*, 519.

22. Martin Luther King, Jr., "I've Been to the Mountaintop," April 3, 1969, recording, 43:07, https://www.americanrhetoric.com/speeches/mlkivebeentothemountaintop.htm.

23. Emma Johnson, "The Real Cost of Your Shopping Habits," *Forbes*, January 15, 2015, https://www.forbes.com/sites/emmajohnson/2015/01/15/the-real-cost-of-your-shopping-habits/.

24. Christine Platt, *The Afrominimalist's Guide to Living with Less* (New York: Simon and Schuster, 2021), 33.

25. Platt, 198.

26. Richard Stearns, *The Hole in Our Gospel* (Nashville: Thomas Nelson, 2009), 266.

27. Grace Holland, *BIC History and Life* 31, no. 2 (August 2008): 254.

28. Susan R. Holman, *God Knows There's Need: Christian Responses to Poverty* (New York: Oxford Press, 2009), 43.

29. Howard Thurman, *Jesus and the Disinherited* (Boston, MA: Beacon Press, 1976), 93.

30. Max Lucado, *Just Like Jesus* (Nashville, TN: Word Publishing, 1998), 34–35.

31. *Evangelical Visitor* 57, no. 24 (November 20, 1944), 14, http://bicarchives.messiah.edu/files/Documents7/1944-11-20_nov_20,1944.pdf.

32. Martin Schrag, *BIC History and Life,* Dec. 1978, 17.

33. Emerson Lesher, *BIC History and Life,* Dec. 1978, 44–45.

34. Harriet Sider Bicksler, "A Missionary's Legacy," *Anabaptist World*, August 11, 2015, https://anabaptistworld.org/a-missionarys-legacy/.

35. Bicksler, "A Missionary's Legacy."

36. Harriet Bicksler, "IMG 0298," July 28, 2015, YouTube video, 2:09, https://www.youtube.com/watch?v=43lGrD66hDo.

CHAPTER 8

1. Bruce Chilton, *Abraham's Curse: Child Sacrifice in the Legacies of the West* (New York: Doubleday, 2008), 178.

2. *Schleitheim Confession*, http://www.anabaptistwiki.org/mediawiki/index.php/Schleitheim_Confession_(source)#cite_ref-35.

CHAPTER 9

1. "Core Values," Brethren in Christ U.S., last modified April 13, 2018, https://bicus.org/about/what-we-believe/core-values/.

2. Tyler Staton, *Praying Like Monks, Living Like Fools: An Invitation to the Wonder and Mystery of Prayer* (Grand Rapids, MI: Zondervan Books, 2022), 47–48.

3. Clinton E. Arnold, *Zondervan Illustrated Bible Backgrounds Commentary: Romans to Philemon, vol. 3* (Grand Rapids, MI: Zondervan, 2002), 351.

4. Arnold, *Zondervan Illustrated Bible Backgrounds Commentary*, 366.

5. Walter Brueggemann, "The Liturgy of Abundance, the Myth of Scarcity," *The Christian Century*, March 24–31, 1999: 342–347.

6. Joshua Nolt, "Finding Rest in a Restless Age," September 16, 2021, https://bicus.org/2021/09/finding-rest-in-a-restless-age/.

7. Donald A. Hagner, *Encountering the Book of Hebrews: An Exposition*, ed. Walter A. Elwell, Encountering Biblical Studies (Grand Rapids, MI: Baker Academic, 2002), 76.

8. Peter Scazzero, *Emotionally Healthy Discipleship* (Zondervan, 2021), 50.

9. *Peaceful Practices: A Guide to Healthy Communication in Conflict* (Akron, PA: Mennonite Central Committee, 2021), 63.

10. Nicholas Kardaras, *Digital Madness: How Social Media Is Driving Our Mental Health Crisis—and How to Restore Our Sanity* (New York: St. Martin's Press, 2022), 22.

11. Eileen Kinch, "Five Things Friday Roundup: Quaker Reflections on Simplicity," *Anabaptist World*, accessed June 30, 2023, https://anabaptistworld.org/five-things-friday-roundup-reflections-on-quaker-simplicity.

12. Kinch, "Five Things Friday Roundup."

CHAPTER 10

1. Luke L. Keefer Jr., "Holiness Affecting Our Witness," *Brethren in Christ History and Life* 31, no. 1 (April 2008): 66.

2. Parker Palmer, *Let Your Life Speak: Listening for the Voice of Vocation* (San Francisco, CA: Jossey-Bass, 2000), 88.

3. Walter Brueggeman, *Sabbath as Resistance* (Louisville, KY: John Knox Press, 2014), 18.

4. Julian of Norwich. *Revelations of Divine Love*, trans. James Walsh (St. Meinrad, IN: Abbey Press, 1974), ch. 32.

5. Martin Buber, *Tales of the Hasidim: The Early Masters* (New York: Shocken Books, 1947), 212.

Contributing Essay Authors

Christina Bosserman (MDiv, PhD) is Lead Pastor at New Vision BIC Church (Pewaukee, Wisconsin) and teaches in the BIC Directed Study Program.

Alan Claassen Thrush (DMin, CFRE) is a minister-on-assignment with MCC since 2006. He belongs to Crest Community BIC Church (Riverside, California).

Rob Douglass (MDiv, PhD) is the pastor of Dillsburg BIC Church (Dillsburg, Pennsylvania).

Lynda Gephart is Pastor of Congregational Life at Harrisburg BIC Church (Harrisburg, Pennsylvania).

Antonio Gonzalez is pastor at BIC Church en Hoyo de Manzanares (Madrid, Spain) and President of BIC Church of Spain.

Hank Johnson (MDiv) is Senior Pastor at Harrisburg BIC Church (Harrisburg, Pennsylvania).

Erica Lloyd is a former BICWM missionary and current volunteer at New Life Community Church (Carlisle, Pennsylvania).

Jonathan Lloyd is a former BICWM missionary and current Director of BIC U.S. World Missions.

Scott MacFeat (MA) is Lead Pastor at Refton BIC Church (Refton, Pennsylvania).

Danisa Ndlovu is former Bishop of BIC Zimbabwe and current volunteer at Faithwalk Ministries International.

Joshua Nolt (DMin) is Senior Pastor at Lancaster BIC Church (Lancaster, Pennsylvania) and teaches in the BIC Directed Study Program.

José Otamendi (MA, SocScD) is Senior Pastor at Jesus Redeemer BIC Church (Caracas, Venezuela).

Naomi Smith is Associate Pastor at Dillsburg BIC Church (Dillsburg, Pennsylvania).

Ryan Stockton (MTS) is Lead Pastor at Marsh Creek Community Church (Exton, Pennsylvania).

The Editors

Terry L. Brensinger is a pastor, writer, and spiritual director who thrives on helping people and churches align with what God is doing in the world. Brensinger received his BA from Messiah College, MDiv from Asbury Theological Seminary, MA in Near Eastern  archaeology from Drew University, and MPhil and PhD in Old Testament studies, also from Drew. The author or editor of four books, Brensinger has pastored three churches, taught at both the university and graduate levels, and served as president of Fresno Pacific Biblical Seminary.

Jennifer Lancaster is the Project 250 coordinator for Brethren in Christ U.S. and adjunct professor at Messiah University. She has a PhD in religion from Temple University. She lives in Lancaster, Pennsylvania, with her husband and daughter, and they attend the Lancaster Brethren in Christ Church.

Alan Robinson is national director of Brethren in Christ U.S. Formerly senior pastor of Carlisle (Pennsylvania) BIC, Robinson lives in Dillsburg, Pennsylvania, with his wife Sharon. They have two adult daughters and two grandchildren.